NEEDLE-MADE RUGS

NEEDLE-MADE RUGS

BY

SIBYL I. MATHEWS

MILLS & BOON LIMITED, LONDON
HEARTHSIDE PRESS, Incorporated, Publishers, NEW YORK

Published by Mills & Boon Limited, 17–19 Foley Street,
London W1A 1DR and Hearthside Press Inc., Publishers,
445 Northern Boulevard, Great Neck, New York 11021

Second Edition 1963
Reprinted (*Revised*) 1967
Reprinted (*Revised*) 1970

ISBN 0.263.70020.8 (Mills & Boon)
SBN 8208.0319.7 (Hearthside)

MADE AND PRINTED IN GREAT BRITAIN
BY JARROLD AND SONS LTD, NORWICH

For

IRENE MILEHAM

With whom I have shared
the pleasures of embroidery for many years,
and whose skilful co-operation has added so much
to the enjoyment of our joint talking
and teaching expeditions

and for

MY HUSBAND

whose help, interest and (above all) patience
have been unfailing
since the days
when the Dragon began it all

Contents

Acknowledgements

WARM thanks are due to those who have helped in the production of this book:

Mrs Addison, Lady Aston, Mrs Elston, Mrs Horton, Mrs Lewis, Mrs Mileham and Mr Ernest Thesiger for lending rugs they have worked to illustrate the use of various stitches and points in design.

Mrs Pontremoli for lending a rug from her own collection.

Mrs Russell for preparing certain charts for the printers.

The National Federation of Women's Institutes and the Committee of *Embroidery* for permission to use some of the text and diagrams from a leaflet and articles written for them by S.I.M.

The Director of the Hôpital St-Jean, Bruges, for permitting the reproduction of the picture by Hans Memlinc (page 113).

The Embroiderers' Guild for permission to use some of the matter written for a Guild Correspondence Course.

My brother, R. A. Hayes, for much help in checking and rechecking the final draft,

and above all

Mrs Harris, A.R.C.A., owing to whose encouragement an idea has developed into a reality and who has most kindly drawn the stitch diagrams that illustrate the text.

S.I.M.

List of Illustrations

HOW IT ALL BEGAN

THAT "Gratitude is the rarest of all the virtues" may be only too true, but possibly it is not always easy to recognise the giver at the time of receiving favours. Certainly it would never have occurred to me in my wildest dreams that when a peculiarly virulent influenza germ attacked my husband it was to be the cause of our acquiring a new pastime the interest and fascination of which would increase as the years went by.

To a man active in mind and body the doctor's dictum that "you cannot go back to work for three or four weeks" was very trying, but the sudden decision to make a rug robbed the time of boredom and ensured a happy convalescence.

My idea of buying a chart from a needlework shop was treated with the scorn which I knew, even then, that it deserved, and I was told that this was going to be "our" rug, not one whose fellow could be met elsewhere.

A dragon of surpassing vitality was transferred from a Chinese plate to half a sheet of notepaper, enlarged, worked out on graph paper, coloured in chalks and finally took shape on canvas, thus beginning the collection of rugs the making of which has given us both twenty-five years of endless amusement.

Knowing nothing of materials or methods of rug making except those advertised so freely, we worked the dragon with a latchet-hook using three holes to the inch canvas (the variety made in white cotton double mesh and divided into squares with a blue line) and in 6-ply Turkey rug wool. Even in those days the cost of such wool seemed great but today it would be trebled.

The dragon was (and is) a delightful creature, in two shades of blue on a cream ground and surrounded by a plain blue border, with black spines, a scarlet tongue and yellow claws, only unluckily he is but a common dragon with three claws instead of being royal with five. Technically he was regrettably bad. With a gauge for cutting the wool into equal lengths and a latchet-hook for pulling the cut lengths through the canvas, it was practically impossible to avoid producing an even pile, but everything else was wrong. The rough, cut edge of the canvas was turned over incorrectly, there was no edging stitch to hold up the pile, and the fact that we had bought too short a length of canvas (penny-wise, pound-foolish) meant that having finished the design we had far too little left for an adequate turn-over at the far end, with the consequence that the edge curled slightly. Such were the penalties of ignorance, and one of the reasons for embarking upon this book is the hope of helping rug makers (especially beginners) to avoid the pitfalls that we have encountered. We have learnt many lessons, chiefly from bitter experience, and we should like others to profit from our mistakes.

Rug making is an intensely individual craft and therefore it is unwise to be dogmatic as regards many of its aspects. Few hard and fast rules have been laid down; stitch directions have been kept as simple as possible consistent with clarity and are illustrated by detailed diagrams at each stage; and all technical suggestions are such as have been tried and found to work satisfactorily, both personally and from the experience of many pupils.

It is hoped that having considered the various types of rugs discussed, and studied the directions for working them, anyone interested in the subject will feel able, without further tuition, to start on a rug that will give much pleasure in the making and will result in the creation of "a thing of beauty".

FIG. 1 *Line drawing of dragon used for the author's first rug.*

Chapter One

RUGS—A HERITAGE FROM THE EAST

THE words "Oriental rugs" can conjure up visions of one of the most beautiful of man's achievements, with the glow of their colouring, the fascinating and intricate patterns used, and, in pile rugs, the sheen that seems to compel the fingers to stroke the surface in order to feel its texture. Among all the marvels poured into the West by the long, winding caravans, none were more wonderful than the "carpets dark as wine". The magic of the East seems to lie in the very names of those carpets—Shiraz, Isphahan, Shirvan, Bokhara, Soumak, Samarkand—they are as colourful as the rugs themselves and surely it must be true that the merchants did not "travel for trafficking alone" but in part appreciated the beauty of what they carried?

Few of us can hope to make "The Golden Journey to Samarkand" and return with bales of wondrous Eastern rugs with which to adorn our homes. But though we cannot travel to the East in reality even a slight knowledge of the story of rugs, their beginnings and their name places can result in a quickening of the imagination and an appreciation of their beauties without which we may glance at them casually but see little.

Anything in the way of a treatise upon such a vast subject as Oriental rugs is, of course, completely outside the scope of this book. There are numerous excellent and erudite works to be enjoyed by all those interested enough to dive into them, and it is hoped that information on simple methods of rug making may arouse such interest. A few gleanings from the fascinating story are, however, not out of place and may enhance the pleasure of the needlewoman (or man) who, admiring Oriental rugs and desiring to possess such beauty, realises how prohibitive is their cost and so starts to make rugs that can be thoroughly satisfying and lovely in their own right, albeit *ersatz* in that they are worked with a needle on a ready-made foundation instead of being hand knotted or woven on a loom.

In the following pages the terms rugs and carpets are used interchangeably. Who can say exactly where one stops and the other starts? It is impossible to differentiate—a covering for the stairs is invariably a "carpet", yet narrow strips quite as long as some stair carpets would be called "rugs".

Floor coverings of a kind must have been one of the earliest comforts of our primitive ancestors, and skins of animals or rushes were probably the first step towards the lush luxury of the modern thick pile all-over floor coverings that we know today.

It is conjectured that the art of carpet making had its earliest beginnings as far back as 5,000 B.C.;[1] mats consisting of a simple weave of warp and weft are shown in paintings in

[1] *Oriental Carpets*, by Sir George Birdwood.

the tombs of the Pharaohs; Albert Achdjian's book *The Rug* has as its first illustration a coloured reproduction of a smooth-faced rug, of the type known as "Kilim", woven in Egypt in the fourth century A.D., which was found in a royal tomb with the colours still bright and clear.

What gives peculiar interest to the study of rugs is the fact that in this age, when everything is pin-pointed and classified to the *n*th degree, nobody so far has discovered for certain when the knotted pile carpet came into existence. Even its place of origin is still doubtful although the general consensus of opinion favours the high land of Asia Minor or Persia.

Necessity frequently breeds invention and as knotted pile carpets are definitely more cosy than the smooth-faced variety, it seems more than probable that they were first made by the nomad tribes of shepherds inhabiting those great plateaux. Their very means of livelihood, their flocks of sheep and goats, were at hand to provide ample wool of a peculiarly strong quality (such as is still produced by flocks pastured in the districts) and it is easy to imagine a weaver of cloth experimenting one day by taking a short twist of wool round two warp threads of his loom and then realising that he had evolved a new technique in his craft. Thus may the pile rug have been born.

A pile rug to form a floor covering, comfortable, warm and as portable as his tent must have seemed an epoch-making discovery to the shepherd, and in time it proved to be so for the world. Once the knotted rug had been invented its supreme efficiency for its purpose made it obvious that its use would spread far and wide, but that use also ensured that but few specimens could, in the nature of things, survive the ages. The marvel is that there are so many lovely rugs, centuries old, to be seen today and it seems likely that we owe their existence to the facts that they were much in demand for use in sacred buildings where they would be treated with care and also that they were frequently used as hangings.

Until lately the oldest pile carpets known were three specimens found in a mosque at Iconium in Asia Minor. From their design it is conjectured that they were made early in the thirteenth century, which would key up as regards date with the known finishing of the building of the mosque.

The recent discovery and opening of five ancient burial mounds in the Pazyrik Valley, in a lonely part of Mongolia, has now brought to light (literally) what is considered to be the oldest existing pile carpet.

The complete contents of these tombs were found to be embedded (and thus preserved) in ice, the reason for this apparently perpetual refrigeration being, so far, left unexplained. Among the numerous exciting finds was a knotted carpet, 6 by 6½ feet, and in excellent condition. The Russian archaeologists who opened up the tombs put the date of the burials at some hundreds of years B.C. and it is from their evidence that this is claimed to be the most ancient pile carpet in the world.

Descriptions of the contents of the tombs, including the carpet, by Mr R. D. Barnett, F.S.A., of the Department of Egyptian and Assyrian Antiquities, British Museum, appeared in the *Illustrated London News* in July 1953 and January 1955, together with coloured photographs. The main colours of the carpet are reds and greenish yellow and they were said to be "gentle"—a pleasant expression with reference to a carpet.

One fact of particular interest is that, although the knot used was in the Turkish tradition as we know it today, other internal evidence points to the rug having been made in Persia. The main border design consists of horses which are being alternately ridden and led, and the horsemen wear characteristic Persian head-dresses. There are griffins in plaques in one of the secondary borders and stags in another, so animals play a large part in the design of this enthralling discovery.

Apart from these unique relics and illustrations in Oriental illuminated manuscripts, our knowledge of the design and colourings of the very old Eastern carpets comes almost entirely from the meticulous work of the great medieval painters. Many rugs appear on their canvases and reappear in much the same form in real life centuries later, and this particular aspect of the fascination of the story of rugs will be discussed further.

It has been said that, in her heyday, Persia achieved perfection in all the arts and her rug making was no exception. The amazing patience and supreme skill shown in some of the rugs that have come down to us are nothing short of miraculous, and we in England are peculiarly fortunate in that we can, merely by visiting the Victoria and Albert Museum during a spare hour when in London, gaze upon one of the most superb of ancient pile carpets. This is the great Ardebil carpet, made for the mosque at Ardebil, a small town in north-west Persia a little to the west of the Caspian Sea and once famed as a place of many pilgrimages. It is "great" in all senses of the word, of wonderful colouring, delicate and elaborate design, measuring 34 feet 6 inches by 17 feet 6 inches and having 340 knots to the square inch, which means about 30 million knots for the whole carpet. It is dated 1540 and its magnificence is of the same calibre as is Rembrandt's *Night Watch* of some 100 years later, a combination of supreme beauty, technical genius and vast size. Hours of inspection of either masterpiece leave much to see and comprehend at another visit.

Probably the flowing lines and perfect curves of the design of the Ardebil carpet are its most striking aspect, and this seeming freedom from the formality imposed by the technique of carpet knotting is characteristic of all the best Persian rugs. It can be achieved only when they are made with many knots to the square inch and with very skilled workmanship. The Persians revelled in such intricacy and their Garden carpets, Hunting carpets, Vase carpets (generic terms for the realistic type of design they favoured), show their supreme genius which has never been surpassed. What could sound more enchanting than The Winter Carpet of the Spring of Chosroes? This was made for Chosroes I, who reigned over Persia from A.D. 531 to A.D. 579 and was so beloved of his people that he was called The Blessed. The tale goes that he loved his garden above all things and had this masterpiece made so that in the winter he could enjoy spring in his palace by means of his Garden carpet.

There is no real demarcation between where the flowing Persian type of carpet ends and the somewhat more conventional Turkish type begins. Wandering tribes took their designs with them and all over the great carpet-making districts somewhat similar designs crop up in slightly new forms.

Religion played a large part in these differentiations. The Persians used figures of men and animals in a delightfully inconsequent manner which made their carpets particularly full of vitality, but the Turks belonged to a more orthodox sect of the Mohammedan faith and their religion forbade them to represent living things on their carpets. In their use of colour similar differences occur. For instance green is used by the Persians but seldom by the Turks because, in addition to representing spring, rebirth and garments worn in Paradise, it is also the sacred colour of the prophet's mantle and, say the Turks, must not be trampled underfoot. Very occasionally it appears in particularly fine prayer rugs as a groundwork colour, the probability being that these were rugs made for very special personages.

Prayer rugs are part of the Moslem's household equipment and small versions of these rugs go with him on his travels, so it is not surprising that many of the loveliest Turkish rugs take this form, with either a single or triple prayer niche at one end, supported by columns and generally with a hanging lamp in the centre. In these rugs the borders are frequently wider than is usual and broken into many "stripes".

For anyone wishing to gain ideas for needle-made rugs a careful study of the Central Asian and Caucasian type of rug is particularly useful, both as regards colour and design, since on the whole these are less elaborate than the Persian and Turkish rugs and their patterns are easier to absorb and adapt for individual needs. In Central Asian rugs great use is made of geometric shapes, octagons, hexagons, diamonds, which make an all-over pattern on the "field" of the rug and are filled with small formal patterns, as are the interstices of the background. The colour schemes are simple, rich reds and browns in several shades always predominating, with blues and whites as secondary colours and occasionally a little green and yellow.

Caucasian rugs are still more geometrical, not to say angular, and even spiky, and are generally characterised by the introduction of entertaining animals—birds, beasts and humans. Their flower and leaf forms are invariably completely stylised and can be adapted and used by the amateur rug maker with extraordinarily good effect.

In time the art of making pile carpets naturally spread both east and west. Indian carpets owe much as regards design to Persian influence, but the Chinese carpets, as might be expected from a nation supremely skilled in all the arts, are unique. They are not generally especially fine as to texture, but their designs and colours, embodying their passion for symbolism, show their superb artistry. It is in China alone that the highly individual "pillar carpets" are made, where the complete form of the rug does not show until the long sides are brought together, when a delightful dragon may be seen wound round a pillar.

When rugs first reached the west they were treated with consummate care and used generally as table coverings (as they are seen sometimes in Holland today). In paintings of the period they appear frequently in such positions and they must have added a feeling of luxury to the cold and dark rooms. Cardinal Wolsey, that knowledgeable "picker-up of unconsidered trifles", managed to acquire a large number of valuable carpets, with which to adorn his new Palace of Hampton Court, by "meeting" the Venetian traders as regards the repeal of the duties on wines imported by them into England. In return for this concession seven "handsome Damascene carpets" arrived in 1519 followed by sixty more a year later, so Wolsey did rather well out of that deal.

Knowledge of carpet-knotting must have percolated into England during the sixteenth century and been practised here, as there are three carpets still in existence known to be of English workmanship and dated 1570, 1584 and 1585 respectively. The fact that carpets were being produced cannot have been widely known, however, as during Queen Elizabeth's reign an attempt was made to find an expert to teach carpet-knotting in this country. A trader sent to the East in 1579 as a representative of the Muscovy Company was thus instructed: "If before you returne you could procure a singular good workeman in the arte of Turkish carpet-making, you should bring the arte into this Realme, and also thereby increase worke to your Company."[1]

A letter from a German visiting England at the end of the century gives yet another proof that the industry was largely unknown as he speaks somewhat scathingly of the Queen's Presence Chamber at Greenwich Palace being strewn with hay, and it is unbelievable that the fashion-conscious Queen would not have acquired carpets if such were being regularly produced and used in her country—or even being imported in appreciable numbers.

Mr Tattersall says that "on looking back it will be seen that there are only known ten complete English carpets that were made before the end of the seventeenth century", but during the seventeenth century itself the Turkey knot was used for numerous small articles of the "canvas work" variety such as cushions. Pile pads for the seat and back of a wooden chair must have been very comforting and maybe they were the forerunners of the stall seats now being worked for so many churches. Twenty such cushions were made between 1660 and 1667 for the Bishop of Ely and bequeathed by him to Pembroke College, Cambridge.

It was towards the end of the eighteenth century that hand-knotted carpet-making became a flourishing industry in England. From that time onwards knotted carpets were produced in several places, Axminster and Wilton being the best known, while considerably later William Morris did much to keep the art alive.

Probably the earliest of all the carpet factories was the one at Wilton and it is only there that hand-knotting has been practised of late years. One of the sad repercussions of this machine age is that 1958 saw the end of this once most flourishing and highly individual business, although machine-made carpets are still being produced at Wilton.

In the East the art continues to employ many people and on the whole the tradition of good workmanship persists, but in Europe generally (with the exception of a comparatively small number of workers producing hand-made carpets in France and Portugal) it is only the amateur who is willing and happy to spend time in such work.

That such time is indeed well employed has been illustrated over and over again, and, whether a rug be coarse or fine, as long as its workmanship and individuality of design and colouring show the same care and patience as that lavished upon the rugs of old, the treasures of the past are not lost but belong to the present.

[1] From Hakluyt's *Voyages*, quoted in Kendrick and Tattersall's *Hand Woven Carpets*.

Chapter Two

MATERIALS AND METHODS

RUG-MAKING materials are of the simplest, but just as the artist needs the best and most suitable paint, canvas and brushes for his particular purpose, so does the creative rug maker need the best wool, canvas and needles. This sounds obvious but it is surprising how often lack of care in the selection of materials ends in much labour being wasted on second-rate results.

Wool

It is essential that this should be of the best quality with no admixture of cotton. Those who tried to make rugs in the late 1940s will remember only too well how impossible it was to produce good ones from the poor post-war so-called wool. The majority of firms now selling rug wool are very reliable but if there is any doubt as to its being pure wool this is easily tested by putting a match to the cut end of a small length—it should smoulder, not burn.

For rugs made on coarse canvas there are many thick wools available, of which that known as "Turkey" wool is the most commonly used and can be bought at nearly all needlework shops. As regards actual thickness, any wool described as "6-ply" should be suitable for a coarse canvas, but Herdwick 3-ply is of equal thickness and Wilton "6-ply" (so-called) is really another thick 3-ply wool (i.e. it is formed of three obviously distinct strands twisted closely together). The selling title of 6-ply is to accord with the popular (if incorrect) idea that the thickness of any wool depends only on the number of plies in it.

The safest guide to the thickness of a wool unknown to the purchaser is, of course, a sample, but the following short list covers the wools mentioned in this book by name, grouped according to their thicknesses. A list of suppliers is given in Appendix 3 at the end of the book.

Thick wool	Turkey 6-ply.
	Wilton "6-ply" (really 3-ply).
	Herdwick 3-ply.
Medium wool	Mixed thrums (generally Axminster) 2-ply.
Fine wool	Brussels thrums (see special description below).
	Crewel wool.

The word "thrums" is an old one and it is interesting to read the advice given by an Elizabethan chronicler to a young venturer to the East at the time when new and exciting textiles were being introduced into England: "In Persia you shall finde carpets of course thrummed wooll, the best of the world, and excellently coloured . . . and you must use meanes to learne all the order of the dying of those thrummes, which are so died as neither raine, wine, nor yet vinegar can staine."[1]

The present-day definition of thrums, according to the dictionary, is "the end of a weaver's thread or any loose thread or fringe" but for rug-making purposes it means the "left-overs" from the carpet factories. As might be expected, therefore, thrums provides excellent material for rugs as regards both colours and wearing qualities and, being waste material (from the point of view of the carpet factories), it is comparatively inexpensive.

Axminster thrums is typical of carpet wool of medium thickness and is, perhaps, the most commonly used wool for needle-made rugs. It is normally 2-ply. In the following pages when the word thrums is used (e.g. two lengths of thrums) it will refer to this particular form of carpet wool.

The thin 2-ply wool, known as "crewel" wool, though available in beautiful colours and of standardised thickness, is expensive and somewhat soft to withstand continual friction if used as the main material of a pile-rug surface. It is, however, useful for adding touches of special colours not otherwise available. There is a less well known 4-ply "crewel" which would also be designated a "fine" wool.

The attractive and inexpensive "Brussels" thrums is very suitable for fine work. It differs from the other wools mentioned in the variety of the forms in which it may be supplied. Some of it may come in simple lengths of 2- or 3-ply wool, varying considerably in thickness, but the majority is usually in the form of loose twists or "tails" of two or more thin strands, each of a 2-ply wool which is very similar to crewel wool in thickness and appearance, though more hairy and generally tougher. The strands in these loose twists can be quickly and easily separated if desired and when separated they will remain as thin straight lengths of 2-ply wool, free from kinks and easy to work with.

An advantage of using a thin wool is that by threading several lengths at once through the needle's eye it can usually take the place of a thicker wool quite successfully. On the other hand, it is laborious to untwist one or more of the closely twisted plies of a thick wool in order to obtain a thinner one, and this procedure is anyhow most inadvisable.

Matching Wool to Foundation

One of the arts of rug making is to ensure an ideal marriage between the wool and the canvas foundation; too little wool will produce a loose and floppy rug and too much bulges the filled holes in the canvas at the expense of the adjoining unfilled holes, making work increasingly difficult and tending to distort the shape of the finished rug and to prevent it lying flat on the floor.

The Farmyard rug (Fig. 2) is an example of an unhappy alliance. This was worked during 1944–5 with various oddments of wool on too soft a piece of canvas (5 holes to the inch). With the rather thick wool, which was all that was available at the time, two lengths used together in the needle proved to be too much for satisfactory working (see above), so a change was made to a single length. This produced a rug which has far too soft a texture

[1] From Hakluyt's *Voyages*, quoted in Kendrick and Tattersall's *Hand Woven Carpets*.

FIG. 2 "Farmyard" rug in Surrey stitch on 5s canvas, designed by G. V. Mathews and worked by Sibyl I. Mathews. Mainly blues and reds with various amounts of other colours, brown outlines. Size 32 × 56 inches.

and will not give the years of hard wear to be expected. What should have been done was to have worked mainly with two lengths in the needle but to have used one length occasionally to stop the cumulative effect of overcrowding every row of holes. This is the procedure advised if some of the wool bought in a bundle of mixed thrums should be rather thicker than the rest—which happens sometimes. The Farmyard rug is an amusing relic of the war years and taught me a never-to-be-forgotten lesson.

Purchasing Wool

Bundles of mixed thrums can be bought at varying prices according to whether the lengths of the wool in the bundles are long, medium or short. At the time of writing, 1967, 6*s*. a lb. is an average price for long lengths.

Wool bought by the hank in one colour is naturally more expensive, and it is a good and economical plan to order a quantity of one or two main colours plus some mixed thrums, which combination can produce excellent results. Some firms will send a selection of wool in several shades of one colour which can be most useful, especially for backgrounds.

For making fine pile rugs Brussels thrums, or "Worsted" as it is listed by some firms, should be used, and either Brussels thrums or crewel wool for fine, smooth-faced rugs. Brussels thrums is at present about 7*s*. to 8*s*. a lb. while crewel wool is about 40*s*. a lb. What should be avoided is so-called "tapestry" wool, sold sometimes for canvas work. It is very soft in texture, frays easily and is quite unsuitable for any type of rug.

When writing for special colours it is a great help to both customers and suppliers if bits of material (any material) are sent as patterns of the colours required. The suppliers then have some guide as to the customer's needs and the latter has cause for a genuine complaint if, for instance, a saxe blue pattern has been sent and a royal blue skein of wool arrives.

Foundation Materials

The true Oriental rug is, of course, worked on a loom, the warp threads being stretched vertically and the weft threads passed horizontally in and out of these. In the pile rugs short pieces of wool are knotted round the warp threads, and, at the end of each row, weft threads are run between the rows to hold them in position. As regards smooth-faced rugs, in Kilims the coloured threads of the pattern actually form the weft, but in Soumaks a weft thread is run between every one or two rows of weaving and does not show on the surface. In all cases the weft threads are well beaten down into place with a tool that some-what resembles a coarse and heavy comb. It will thus be seen that the warp and weft threads of a loom-made rug become an integral part of it as work proceeds, but when a rug is to be worked comfortably on the knees with a needle it is necessary to use a ready-made foundation. The threads of this foundation, which run parallel to the long and short sides of the rug, will still be called the warp and weft respectively. Also the warp threads will be described as "vertical" and their ends as the "top" and "bottom" of the foundation, corresponding with their positions in a loom although the foundation actually lies horizontally on the worker's knees.

As with the wool the selection of the foundation material is important and demands forethought, particularly if a fine rug is attempted. In this case it is advisable to use a linen rather than a cotton canvas (the usual material of which rug canvas is made) owing to its greater strength and longer wearing qualities.

The foundation may be of either of two types:

1. *Double mesh canvas*, which can be obtained to give 3, 4, 5, 7, 8, 9, 10 (or more) holes to the inch. For the sake of brevity these canvases will be referred to in future as 3s, 4s, 5s, etc.

In double mesh canvas the threads of the warp, and usually of the weft, are arranged in "double bars", i.e. pairs of threads comparatively close together alternating with obvious "holes"—for example see Fig. 3 on page 31. But occasionally with the fine linen canvases, still ranked as double mesh, only the warp threads are arranged in obvious double bars, all the weft threads being evenly spaced though with the same total number of threads per inch as in the warp. For such canvas, each pair of successive weft threads must be treated as one double bar of weft for working purposes and when counting "holes" along the direction of the warp (i.e. between the weft threads) only every other space between the threads must be counted.

2. *Single mesh canvas* has both warp and weft threads equally spaced, and for working purposes each pair of successive threads, whether of warp or weft, is treated as one double bar of double mesh canvas, except where otherwise stated hereafter. For single mesh canvas an evenly woven jute (see Fig. 6 on page 35), is recommended which gives 8 threads to the inch (corresponding to 4 bars to the inch of the double mesh). It has the advantage that it is very pleasant to handle, being of a comparatively pliable texture albeit very strong, but counting its threads is more of a strain than with the double mesh type, a material factor for those who have somewhat imperfect eyesight and take up rug making as an interesting and restful hobby. From the Otterburn Mills, Carlisle, come two other jutes known as Patterdale canvas, one (quality A) giving about 7 and the other (quality B) only about 4 threads to the inch.

It should be noted that the cut edges of all these single mesh materials fray very easily and must be secured by two or three rows of machine stitching before any other work is started.

Although excellent pile rugs can be made on these jutes and they are satisfactory for most varieties of smooth-faced rugs, some of the flat stitches are far better worked on double mesh canvas.

There is also a somewhat stiff single mesh "open" canvas to be had which is suitable for certain flat stitches only.

Both double and single mesh canvases are obtainable in any length and in various widths between the "selvedges" (i.e. the finished edgings of extra close warp threads where the weft threads stop and double back on themselves). The range of widths starts at 12 inches and 48 inches is the maximum except on very rare occasions, and not all canvases can be bought in all widths. As with wool, it is wise to ask for patterns before ordering canvas.

The following table is given as a guide for the correct thickness of wool to use with the various foundation canvases.

Double Mesh Canvas	Suitable amount of wool to use in the needle
3 holes to the inch	One length of 6-ply or three lengths of thrums.
4 holes to the inch	Two and sometimes three lengths of thrums (depending on the thickness of the wool).
5 holes to the inch	Two or sometimes one length of thrums (depending on the thickness of the wool).
7 holes to the inch	One length of thrums, five strands of Brussels thrums or five lengths of 2-ply crewel wool or two lengths of 4-ply crewel wool.
8 holes to the inch	Three or four strands of Brussels thrums or an equal number of lengths of 2-ply crewel wool.
9 holes to the inch	Two or three strands of Brussels thrums or an equal number of lengths of 2-ply crewel wool or one length of 4-ply crewel wool.
10 holes to the inch	Two strands of Brussels thrums or two lengths of 2-ply crewel wool.

Single mesh canvas	
8 threads to the inch jute, equals 4s double bar canvas	Two and sometimes three lengths of thrums (depending on the thickness of the wool).
Patterdale canvas A	Two and sometimes three lengths of thrums (depending on the thickness of the wool).
Patterdale canvas B	One length of 6-ply wool. This canvas is very loosely woven and has to be used with great care or it pulls out of shape.

Single mesh "open" stiff canvas	
7 threads to the inch	Two lengths of thrums.
10 threads to the inch	One length of thrums.

This table does not pretend to be infallible. Wools of a given make and description may still vary somewhat in thickness; also on a given canvas thicker wool can be used for some kinds of stitch than for others. Therefore the only safe way to settle whether a certain wool or combination of wools is suitable for the canvas to be used is to try it out on a small and (roughly) square area of the canvas. Careful note should be taken as to whether the canvas threads of the worked area are completely covered without the filled holes being so over-crowded as to cramp the unfilled holes bordering the area. The working of a sampler is in any case strongly to be recommended both for a check-up on the general colour scheme proposed and also to gain complete mastery of the stitches.

Needles

These should be blunt-pointed and sufficiently large for the wool used to slip easily through the eye.

People vary slightly as regards their preference for a coarser or finer needle, but sizes

14 to 16 are advised for coarse canvas, sizes 18 to 22 for 7s and 8s canvas and size 22 for 9s or 10s canvas.

Some workers like to use a blunt-pointed raffia needle for the coarser canvases.

Methods

Rugs worked with a needle on a ready-made foundation fall into two categories—pile and smooth-faced—and it is difficult to say which type can exercise the greater fascination on the maker. That being so, beginners are advised to try out both types, and, if they have the energy, different methods of producing the same type, either on a sampler (as previously suggested) or on a set of small mats, before embarking on a big rug. This is especially advisable if the ambitious wish to make a fine rug as their first large one.

To produce a really beautiful rug is supremely worth while but it cannot be done unless the worker is prepared to take a considerable amount of time and trouble over its accomplishment. No good rug can be completed in a few hours; hence the importance of careful planning and selection of the method to be used as well as of the right materials.

Once the work has been started the somewhat mechanical action of the technique, particularly in the pile rugs, is immensely soothing, and as the pattern grows the interest becomes greater as each row is completed. It is not fortuitous that it is one of the great stand-bys of the occupational therapists in their work of rehabilitation. Many personal experiences have proved the value of rug making from the "escapist" point of view. It employs the hands in a rhythmical, easy way, and also the head to whatever extent is desired, the latter depending upon the complexity or simplicity of the design and colouring used.

Pile Rugs

Two methods are advocated for these—Surrey stitch and Ghiordes or Turkey knot—both of which produce an excellent short pile.

On the surface they are indistinguishable, although somewhat different on the back, and the choice is purely a matter of personal preference based on the actual action of working the stitch.

The method by which a gauge is used to enable wool to be cut into even lengths of about $2\frac{1}{2}$ inches, plus a latchet-hook with which to push these pieces of wool through the canvas and knot them, is still that most commonly practised for hand-made rugs. It produces a somewhat long but even pile and such rugs are very durable, but the latchet-hook involves the use of a large mesh canvas with either 6-ply wool or its equivalent in thrums. Anything thinner will result in a poor pile on such coarse canvas. This naturally means an expensive rug—as was the dragon—and if short pile is used, on a finer canvas and requiring less wool, a rug will be made of the same size at an appreciably lower cost and with a more attractive texture. On the other hand an advantage of the gauge-hook method is that an area of a given size can be filled much more rapidly with 6-ply wool on 3s canvas than with thrums on 5s canvas, and there will always be devotees of this method. Short pile rugs, however, are more interesting to make as skill is needed to ensure that the pile is of even texture, and time has proved that they will wear equally well.

Many people start their rug-making careers using the gauge-hook method and afterwards try the needle, and I have yet to come across anyone who, having made the change, would willingly revert to the hook.

Smooth-Faced Rugs

For these a great many of the canvas work stitches are suitable and from the personal experience of many workers the following are selected as being particularly satisfactory, taking into consideration wear and ease of working as well as appearance:

> Cross stitch
> Long-legged cross stitch
> Rice stitch
> Tent stitch
> Interlocking Gobelin stitch
> French stitch
> Soumak stitch.

This list does not pretend to be exhaustive. There are other stitches which can be, and have been, used for making rugs, and those who are or who become experts will find plenty of scope for experimenting with stitches, especially if they study Mary Thomas's *Dictionary of Embroidery Stitches.*

Except for French stitch all those listed above have one thing in common, viz. that they slope diagonally across the threads in the front of the canvas, therefore ensuring that it is well and truly covered—provided of course that enough wool has been used in the needle. Stitches that follow straight lines parallel to the threads of the canvas nearly always show the canvas and are therefore unsatisfactory. The reason that French stitch is adequate is that in the working every hole is entered four times, the stitches are tied down very tightly, and packed so closely together that the canvas is of necessity well covered.

Of the rugs illustrated, all of which are made in either one or a combination of these stitches, many have already been in use for some years and have proved their workaday qualities.

The methods of working the various stitches, both pile and flat, are applicable to either coarse or fine canvas. All of them can be used on either double or single mesh canvas foundation, but the double mesh is strongly advised for French and Soumak stitch because the stitches can be counted with far greater ease when worked on the double mesh.

Weight of Wool for a Rug

It is impossible to estimate the weight of wool required for a needle-made rug with a close degree of accuracy owing to the number of factors involved, including the human one. All that can be done is to give a rough guide based on the two most important of these, viz. size of canvas mesh and nature of rug (i.e. whether smooth-faced or pile).

Taking smooth-faced rugs first, the larger the mesh, the thicker must be the amount of wool carried in the needle to hide the canvas threads and therefore the thicker and heavier will be the layer of wool covering on both the front and back of the finished rug. Again the stitch used also has an effect on the weight of wool required, mainly owing to the proportion of wool used up at the back of the canvas. For example, rice stitch uses a lot more wool than Soumak stitch.

With pile rugs, the weight of wool must clearly depend on the length of pile chosen by the individual worker but the *minimum* length for safety against knots working loose will again depend on the size of the mesh and the corresponding amount of wool carried in the needle—see table on page 25.

A factor affecting both types of rug is the intricacy of the pattern, since wherever a new colour is started wool is wasted—particularly in smooth-faced rugs—so that intricate patterns waste more than simple ones. It may be added that a beginner is likely to waste more wool than an experienced worker.

The number of different colours used must also be taken into consideration as regards waste. A complicated pattern might be worked in very few colours but many colours mean many skeins of wool and all of these are unlikely to be exactly used up.

The table below is based on the average weight of wool in a number of rugs worked in various stitches, waste and variation of stitch, etc., being allowed for by an ample margin of error so that the figures should be on the high side especially for Soumak stitch.

It must again be emphasised that no table can give more than a rough guide.

Holes per inch in the canvas	Type of stitch	Approximate number of ounces of wool per square foot
3	Long pile using 6-ply wool	11 oz.
4	Short pile using thrums	8 oz.
4	Smooth-faced (flat stitches) using thrums	7 oz.
5	Short pile or smooth-faced using thrums	6 oz.
7 to 10	Either short pile or smooth-faced (see page 25 for suitable wool).	$5\frac{1}{2}$ oz.

It is a surprising fact that on the finer canvases, whether the stitch is pile or flat makes comparatively little difference provided that the length of the pile is not out of proportion to the thickness of the wool used.

If too much wool is ordered it will be seldom that the surplus cannot be worked into a later rug, while if a colour runs out before a rug is finished and cannot be matched exactly, it is only in the best Oriental tradition to use one or more changes of shade (within reason) in the middle of an area of one general colour. In fact, as will be further discussed in Chapters Five and Seven, changes or "breaks" in background colour are frequently made deliberately to avoid a monotonous appearance. However there are, of course, types of design in which such breaks are undesirable and where this is likely to be so, it is wise to err on the side of over-estimating when ordering wool.

The Use of Fine Canvas

Naturally the finer the work the longer it takes to produce a rug, and probably the majority of people will be well advised to start with a moderately coarse canvas, say 5s, and then, if filled with enthusiasm, to embark upon one needing greater effort. It is generally men who will begin by making a rug on 8s or finer canvas with perfect complacency and will produce quite beautiful results.

A good half-way house is 7s canvas and when once "bitten" by the fascination of doing a fine rug it is difficult to return to the quicker, coarser canvases although for practical use these are admirable. It is all a question of temperament—some people will prefer to take three or four years over one piece of fine work while others would rather make three or four rugs in the same time—and both the actual stitches recommended and the suggestions for designing home-made rugs are based on the various preferences of rug makers in general who wish to use their needles. The ideas for designing apply largely to rugs made with the gauge-hook method also.

The question of the type of canvas to use is summed up very neatly by Mr C. E. C. Tattersall in his invaluable little book *Notes on Carpet-Knotting and Weaving*:

> The labour of making a carpet depends rather on the number of knots it contains than on its actual size, and so wide is the variation of texture that one carpet may entail more than twenty times the work of another of similar dimensions. There is little advantage in pushing the fineness very far. Pleasing textures can be obtained with 25 knots to the square inch; 50 will meet all ordinary requirements; while 100 may be regarded as the limit that can be reached under Western ideas of the value of time.

Chapter Three

PREPARATION OF CANVAS AND TREATMENT OF EDGES

APART from the use of the best materials, the correct treatment of the edges of the canvas foundation will do more than anything else to ensure the long life of a rug, while also adding to its pleasing appearance. By far the greatest wear and tear comes upon the edges, and if these are not strengthened the tufts of a pile rug soon tend to lie down flat near the edges, and in both pile and smooth-faced rugs the selvedges can disintegrate with startling rapidity. Bitter personal experience emphasised this as the selvedges of the Dragon rug referred to in the Preamble to this book began to fray after it had been in use for some years and repairing it neatly proved to be a most tiresome job.

Before starting for the first time on a full-sized rug it is most desirable to practise on a sampler, both in respect of the necessary treatment of the canvas edges and of trying out alternative rug stitches. A yard of 12 or 18 inch wide double mesh canvas—preferably 5s but failing that 4s—should be enough for three samplers, one of which can in due course be used for the pile stitches described in the next chapter and the others for the various flat stitches described in Chapters Five and Six. Such samplers can serve as a useful book of reference in the future.

For those who prefer to work on jute or some other form of single mesh canvas, that material should, of course, be used for a preliminary sampler. Double mesh canvas is, however, strongly advised for a beginner and *this type of canvas will be assumed hereafter except where single mesh canvas (jute, etc.) is specifically mentioned.*

Although the instructions which follow relate to a full-sized rug, they apply equally to the preliminary sampler except where the context obviously precludes this.

Preparation of Canvas

Whatever type of canvas is used the cut ends must be dealt with without delay or they will fray, this (as has already been mentioned) being particularly the case with the single mesh jute. At the end where the rug is to be started the cut edge should be folded over for 2 to $2\frac{1}{2}$ inches (1 inch will serve for a sampler) when using canvas having up to 5 holes to the inch, or 1 to $1\frac{1}{2}$ inches for finer canvases, and should then be oversewn firmly to the canvas, making sure that each hole in the turn-over lies exactly above the corresponding hole beneath it since the rug is begun through the resulting double thickness of canvas, see Fig. 3. When using double mesh canvas a double bar of the weft threads dividing the

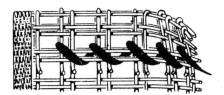

F IG . 3   *Double canvas turn-over.*

holes *must* form each of the two extreme ends of the rug, (this is important if a neat edge is to result, see above, Fig. 3), and for a single mesh foundation two successive weft threads of the material must do so. A complete cross stitch is the strongest method of doing the oversewing (see Fig. 4 below), and it is worth the time it takes for the strength of the result it produces. It is very annoying if the cut edge should start to fray out owing to inadequate oversewing before the "double" has been worked.

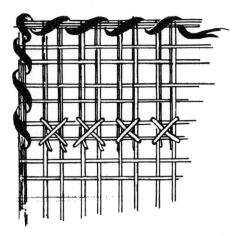

F IG . 4   *Corner point and oversewing*
"double" with cross stitches.

The far end of the canvas should be oversewn roughly along its cut edge to prevent initial fraying (machining is best for single mesh jute) and left thus until the rug is nearing completion, when the exact number of rows still needed for finishing the design can be checked and the canvas folded over and sewn down in the correct position.

When starting to work a pile rug, the fold-over should be on the front face of the canvas where the pile will hide the little cut ends which always protrude through the oversewing however closely it has been worked. On the other hand when starting a smooth-faced rug the fold should be a fold-under, i.e. it should come underneath since this minimises the liability of a slight ridge to show where the canvas changes from double to single thickness, especially where a fine canvas is worked with correspondingly thin wool.

Edging Stitch

Next in priority to securing the cut ends comes the consideration of how to cover the edges of the canvas. There are several possible methods of doing this but of these the plaited edging stitch alone will be described as it has been found by the majority of workers to be the most generally satisfying. There are sound reasons for this preference:

(*a*) It is extremely strong and hard wearing.
(*b*) It is simple to work.
(*c*) It looks well and thus adds to the attractive appearance of the finished rug, although
(*d*) it is not obtrusive and therefore liable to detract from the rug itself.
(*e*) Finally, a great advantage of this stitch is that if, due to accident or long service, the rug shows signs of wear, it is particularly easy to repair.

As pile stitches will be considered before those for smooth-faced rugs, it would be as well to assume that the sampler to be worked first is for pile stitches. That being so the plaited edging stitch, or plait as it will usually be called, should be started at the top right-hand corner hole of the sampler with the cut edge uppermost. The needle is successively:

1. brought from the back of the canvas leaving 2 or 3 inches of the tail end of the wool lying along the top edge (where it can be held by the free hand) to be covered by subsequent stitches;
2. brought through the next hole to the left (again from back to front);
3. taken back to the original hole a second time (thus forming a cross stitch over the top of the canvas);
4. carried forward 3 holes, i.e. leaving out holes 2 and 3;
5. taken back 2 holes to hole 2.

The plait is then continued—always on 3 holes and back 2 holes, i.e. missing 2 holes on the forward stitch and 1 on the backward stitch and never forgetting that the needle should pass always from the back to the front of the canvas.

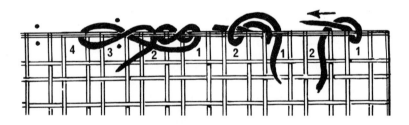

FIG. 5   *Plaited edging stitch.*

Fig. 5 illustrates three stages of the stitch; the right-hand one shows the first half of the initial cross stitch and how the tail of the wool is to be tied down along the top canvas bar; the next shows the completion of the cross stitch; and the left-hand one shows the "on 3 back 2" as well as the completed initial cross stitch. In the last the tail of the wool has now been bound behind the top canvas bar and so is invisible.

In the diagrams the plait is shown being worked over only one double bar, such as should form the top edge of the sampler or a rug when a narrow edge is wanted. In this case when the plait starts down the selvedge edge the latter should be doubled back underneath the canvas to half its width throughout its length so that the plaits along the ends and sides of the work come out about the same width. With a pile rug this turn-back is on the opposite side of the canvas to the turn-overs of the cut ends. If a slightly wider edge is preferred, the plait can be worked over a complete hole of the canvas (which includes two bars instead of just the end one shown in the diagram) and when the selvedge is reached this is not doubled back and the whole width of it is covered so that again the top and bottom and side edges will match in width.

As the plait arrives at the top left-hand corner, the stitch must be "shortened" thus. When "on 3" finishes in the corner hole it should be followed by "back 2", on 2, back 1, on 1, so that the last stitch as well as the first along the edge is a simple cross stitch.

Next the corner should be oversewn as neatly as possible (see below for further details) and the plait started down the selvedge edge, beginning with a simple cross stitch, the first half of which should be made in the direction in which the plait is to be worked. It is generally advisable to use a greater total thickness of wool in the needle (say three lengths instead of two) when working wide plaits, e.g. the "complete hole" top edge and the complete unfolded selvedges which go with it.

The foregoing directions are for a plaited edging stitch worked from right to left, but it is just as easy to do it from left to right. In this case the first half of the first cross is made from left to right, the needle is taken back to the original hole and then continues its journey by going on 3 holes to the right, etc.

When a new length of wool is needed the tail of the old one is brought out at the long stitch (the "on 3" hole) and left loose, the new one is threaded along the back of the worked plait for a short distance and brought out at the same (long stitch) hole, and then the plait is continued as before. The loose tail of the old length is carried along the top of the canvas until it is covered, and it should be impossible to tell where the join has been made if these directions are carried out carefully and no difference made in the tension of the plait.

It is important to remember that:

1. Needlessly long lengths of wool should be avoided, about $2\frac{1}{2}$ feet being ample. People have been known to use yards of wool in order to avoid having to make a join; this is unwise.

2. When two or three lengths of wool are being used together in the needle these must lie neatly side by side along the edge, and a frequent turn of the needle will keep the wool from twisting and ensure the desired flat appearance of the plait. Attention to this small detail will make all the difference to the look of the finished edge.

3. The needle eye should ideally be moved along the wool every few stitches in order to avoid "roughing it up", so it is better to use two lengths rather than one long length doubled. Since, however, this procedure entails pulling four thicknesses of wool through the holes, the latter method is the lesser of two evils if the wool is rather thick. The same thing applies to the way in which the wool should be threaded through the needle when it comes to working the main rug stitches.

Covering the Corners

The obvious difficulty regarding this (or any other) edging is how to cover the sharp points when arriving at the corners.

There is no certain and simple rule for obtaining a perfect result and to a considerable extent trial and error is necessary—and of course practice. Some correspondence pupils of the writer volunteered the information that they began to feel satisfied with their results after working about twelve sampler corners! This is a counsel of perfection and many people can produce excellent corners after working three or four on a sampler. While, however, the way to success offers a wide scope for individual originality, the following device has proved useful for helping to solve this tiresome problem. It can be tried out on the two bottom corners of the sampler of which only the top edge and part of a selvedge have perhaps been worked.

Before any plait arrives at or is started from a particular corner, put a dab of paint, stain or dye on the corner point of the canvas of the same colour, as nearly as possible, as the wool used for the plait. (Ink is very satisfactory for use with dark blue wool.) When the paint is dry, and using the same wool as for the intended plait, oversew the canvas edge with simple sloping stitches from a few holes one side of the corner to a few holes the other side, being careful to include one stitch directly over the corner point—see Fig. 4, page 31. This latter stitch is unlikely to stay in place when the sampler has been handled but it can be pushed back into position and held there while it is being oversewn by the plait in due course.

An alternative to the row of sloping stitches is to work a single cross stitch *exactly* across the corner point and in order to hold it in position to pierce the first half of it with the needle when working the second half. Both starting and finishing tails of the wool used for this special corner cross stitch must of course be firmly secured in some suitable manner.

When the corner is being finally oversewn it will be found that the presence of a special corner stitch provided by either of the above ways is surprisingly helpful. The paint, of course, merely camouflages any small bit of the canvas point that insists on showing itself despite all efforts.

When working the narrow type of edge the special stitch across the corner helps to hold down the folded selvedge there as well as enabling the point to be more adequately covered.

In order to avoid the somewhat thick edge where the selvedge fold-over meets the fold of the cut end (resulting in four thicknesses of selvedge), a small piece of the selvedge can be cut away where it will be seen to protrude beneath the turn-over, but this must be done with great care and the cut must not be taken right up to the corner.

Treatment of Edges of Pliable Single Mesh Canvas

The majority of experienced rug makers consider that the foregoing method of dealing with the edge is the best, whatever type of canvas is used, but when using single mesh jute the following are possible alternatives to the plaited edging stitch:

    1. Double crochet.

2. Blanket stitch.
3. Twisted cable stitch.

The working methods for all these can be found in Mary Thomas's *Dictionary of Embroidery Stitches*. With any of them the stitches should be worked between every thread of the canvas and about 3 or 4 threads deep.

For those who wish to use the plaited edging stitch for single mesh jute but who wilt at the thought of working through the recommended 2 inches of "double" there are two popular variations.

1. Turn over a width of 4 threads at the ends, machine these firmly down on to the canvas below them with several rows of stitching and then work each plait as in Fig. 5 but covering the whole wide turn-over instead of only one double bar of double mesh canvas as in Fig. 5. With this method the selvedge is also turned over to the same depth and at the corners the turn-over of the cut edge and the selvedge are mitred to meet at an angle of 45 degrees, see Fig. 6. The plait is then continued over the whole turn-over (as at the ends) in the usual way, remembering always that in following along the edge, two of the single threads equal one double bar of the other type of canvas. The result looks well and many rug makers advocate this procedure when using jute, but it stands to reason that a rug will have a longer life if there is the 2-inch double to take the extra wear on its ends.

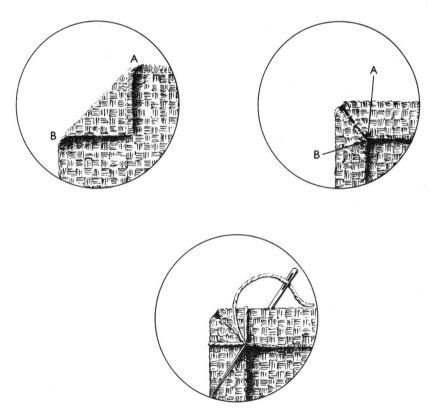

FIG. 6 *Jute canvas, mitred corner.*

2. Another method of making a strong wide edge with jute is to machine it several times along its rough edge and then, instead of turning it over, to work the plait stitch *twice* directly over this cut edge, first over 2 threads and then over 4, so that the deep plait covers the narrow one. With this method the needle is passed between *every* thread of the canvas instead of between every two threads. It is, of course, most essential that all 4 threads of the canvas should be well caught in the machining, especially the first two. A single length of 2-ply thrums is recommended for this edge.

Width of Edging

The width of canvas over which the edging stitch is worked is purely a matter of personal preference and the three different widths which have been suggested may be summarised thus, the plait along the cut ends in each case approximating in width to that along the selvedge sides:

1. For double mesh canvas with folded selvedges, the end plaits should be worked over the one double bar only as shown in the edging stitch diagrams. It will be about one-eighth of an inch wide, varying according to the wool thickness.

2. For double mesh canvas with unfolded selvedges the end plait should be worked over one row of complete holes (two double bars) giving a width of about a quarter of an inch for 5s canvas, say, and of course varying with the canvas.

3. For single mesh jute canvas with the usual 8 threads to the inch, end plaits should be over 4 threads (half an inch) and side plaits should be made of approximately equal width.

Completion of Edging in Stages

The edging is closely bound up with the finishing as well as the beginning of a rug. For a pile rug, as long as the worker is not liable to pull the rug out of shape in the making (as are some otherwise excellent workers), the following procedure has been found to be satisfactory.

1. Turn over and sew down the two cut edges of the canvas, one roughly (see page 31) and the other properly as in Fig. 4.

2. Work the sloping stitch (Fig. 4) over the two corners at each end of this latter edge.

3. With this edge at the top and the correct side of the canvas uppermost, begin the plaited edge stitch at the right-hand corner (it will cover part of the sloping stitch already worked), work from right to left all along the top edge, round the left-hand corner and carry the plait a few inches down the left-hand selvedge.

4. Start again at the right-hand corner and work the plait a few inches down the right-hand selvedge.

This method makes a strong framework for the start of the rug and the plait should be continued at intervals down the sides of the rug so that it is always a short way in front of the pile after that has been begun, see Fig. 7 opposite where a short pile, striped rug has just been started on jute to show this method of procedure.

When the rug is nearing completion, the far, cut edge should be doubled over at the correct canvas bar and sewn down properly. The sloping stitch should then be worked

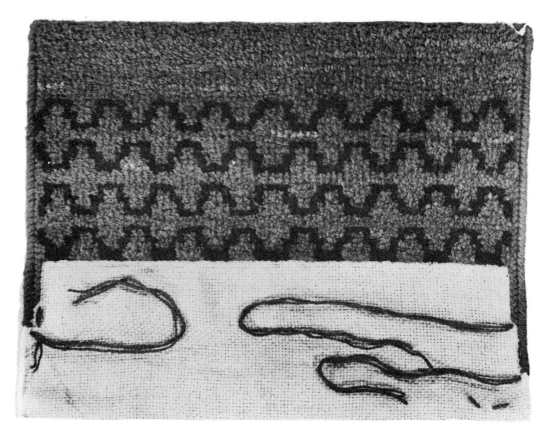

FIG. 7   *Red and black rug in Surrey stitch, on 4s jute canvas, unfinished to show progress of edging stitch.   About half the area of the rug is visible.*

over the last two corners and the plait finished along one selvedge, taken round the corner and along the last edge. The other selvedge plait is continued and they meet at the last corner. This has been found to be a better method than attempting to work the whole edge before beginning the rug, in which case the last edge cannot be adjusted in case of error. Also the gradual growth of the framework helps to keep the whole rug in good shape during working.

Where smooth-faced rugs are concerned, or if the pile worker knows himself or herself to be inclined to pull the rug out of shape, stretching will eventually be necessary and it is better to leave *all* the edging (except the sloping stitches used to prepare the first two corners), to be worked after the rest of the rug is completed and stretched—see Chapter Ten for details of this process. Although a smooth-faced rug may be of perfect shape when finished, its appearance is invariably improved by damping and stretching; hence the suggestion that for *all* smooth-faced rugs the edging stitch should be left until afterwards.

The above considerations do not, of course, apply to small samplers used for practising the stitches and for seeing how the rest of the rug links up with the edging stitch.

Chapter Four

SHORT PILE RUGS—SURREY STITCH AND GHIORDES KNOT

PILE rugs are started just inside the edging stitch (with the turned-over cut edge upper-most) and with the full length of the canvas stretching *away* from the worker. This applies to whichever of these two stitches is used.

For left-handed workers it is naturally easier to do the stitch in the opposite direction to that described and other instructions hereafter will need corresponding modifications, as experience will show.

When single mesh canvas is used for the foundation, two threads equal the double bar of the double mesh canvas as previously stated.

Many people consider that a pile rug is improved if a row of long-legged cross stitch is worked between the edging stitch and the start of the pile. This point is dealt with fully in Chapter Five on page 45.

Surrey Stitch

This stitch owes its name to the fact that it was first evolved by Mrs Hawker Smith, a member of a Surrey Women's Institute. There is a great fascination in its actual working and it makes a particularly strong, hard-wearing rug owing to the fact that each stitch covers the foundation in two different directions, vertically and horizontally, and that every hole is entered four times. An added attraction is the reverse side of the rug where the pattern shows up with startling clarity and exquisite neatness.

Each pile stitch or knot is made with two movements of the needle, the first being to-wards the worker and the second from right to left at right angles to the first movement.

For the sake of clarity the correct order in which the needle should pass through the holes of the canvas from the front or the back is indicated by numbers in the majority of the diagrams that illustrate the stitches throughout this book. The canvas represented on all the diagrams is double mesh.

1st Movement (Fig. 8A and Fig. 8B). The needle is brought under a double weft bar of the canvas towards the worker from hole 1 to hole 2 and the wool drawn through until only a length a little more than the required length of the pile is left—say three-quarters of an inch (see opposite). The needle is then carried up to the left of this short end and the latter is brought straight down over the bar, the left thumb being placed on it at 5 to hold it firm.

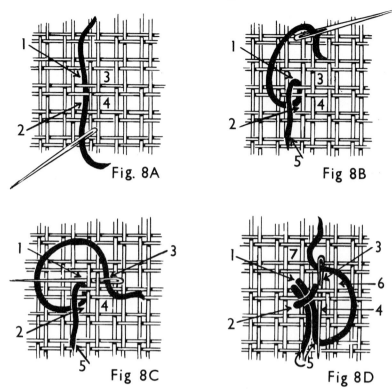

FIG. 8 *Working of Surrey stitch.*

2nd Movement (Fig. 8C). The needle is inserted at hole 3, and brought out at hole 1, passing *over* the loop of wool. The needle is then drawn down and pulled towards the worker, when it will be found that a knot has been made on top of the canvas. The wool is then cut to the required length of the pile (say three-quarters of an inch) unless the same colour is to be used in the next stitch. In the latter case the needle is passed under the bar of canvas between holes 3 and 4 (Fig. 8D) and through the loop of wool which will thereby have been produced. The needle is drawn through until the loop is the length of the required pile. The loop is then held down firmly with the left thumb (at 5, Fig. 8D), the wool is carried upwards as in Fig. 8B and the second movement of the stitch completed as before (i.e. from 6 to 3, Fig. 8D). As long as the stitches are to be all of one colour the loops are continued along the row in this way, but every time a single stitch of a new colour is needed the method of procedure is that illustrated in Fig. 8A to C.

For the second and following rows the needle is inserted under the bar of the canvas immediately above the last completed row, as from 7 to 1 (Fig. 8D).

Length of Pile. The length of three-quarters of an inch suggested above is suitable for canvas meshes of 3 to 4 holes to the inch, but when finer canvas is used this length should be proportionally reduced.

It may be helpful to note that the loops really consist of two blanket stitches, one towards the worker that is *not* pulled tight followed by one horizontally from right to left that *is* pulled tight. Remembering this will ensure that the needle always passes *over* the wool when forming the second part of the stitch—a fact that is sometimes forgotten with the result that the knot is not tied correctly.

Turkey or Ghiordes Knot

Takes its name from Ghiordes, a village in Asia Minor famous for its weaving and rugs, and it can be reproduced with a needle to give exactly the same knot as when worked with the fingers on a loom. It is also interesting to note that a machine has now been invented which reproduces the knot very faithfully in machine-made carpets and rugs.

It is worked over the two adjacent threads forming each double bar of warp or, if a single mesh canvas is used, over the warp threads in pairs. Being worked in one direction only, it cannot be quite as strong on the back as Surrey stitch where the threads of the canvas are pulled together in two directions, nor does it produce such an attractive pattern on the reverse side of the rug. There are, however, many people who prefer the action of working always in one direction (and say that they find it rather quicker in execution than Surrey stitch) while, as previously mentioned, on the front the two methods give an exactly similar appearance.

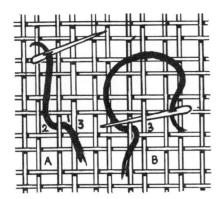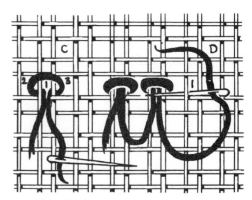

FIG. 9   *Working of Turkey or Ghiordes knot.*

1st Movement. To work the stitch on double mesh canvas, the needle is inserted downwards between the two bars, round the back of the left-hand one and brought up again, leaving the short tail end held down by the left thumb as in Surrey stitch.

2nd Movement. The needle is then taken across the front of both bars, down and under round the right-hand one, and brought up again between the two bars, when the resulting knot is pulled tight.

Note that the start and finish of the stitch is thus between the same two threads of a double bar.

In Fig. 9A to D the complete working of the stitch is shown in both its stages.

As with Surrey stitch the wool is cut off after the first stitch in a row if a new colour is needed and the same process repeated, otherwise the worker proceeds along the row leaving the resultant loops to be cut later. The second row follows on above the next double weft bar, i.e. the warp bars only are used and the double weft bars are left bare.

In both pile methods the loops should be cut as each row is completed. If several rows are worked before any loops are cut the odds are that many of them will be missed, and it is extraordinary how these show up when the rug is finished. Even when cutting row by row it is easy to miss a loop occasionally, therefore this regular cutting is important or numerous odd loops will affect the finished look of the pile.

It is advisable to work in straight rows across the width of the canvas from left to right, completing each row before beginning the next. This helps to ensure that the canvas does not pull out of the straight and, if a chart is used, that this is followed correctly. Although experienced rug makers sometimes work in blocks of a few rows this can lead to trouble with an intricate pattern and the scheme is not recommended.

An artificial gauge of any kind is quite unnecessary, in fact it is rather a nuisance, and the worker very rapidly gains mastery over the required length of the loops and the experience needed to vary this according to the size of the foundation, i.e. whether coarse or fine. It has already been stated that the coarser the canvas the longer should be the loop and resultant pile. If any help is needed, settling the left thumb comfortably into each loop as the work proceeds makes a good natural gauge of length when using the coarser canvases (although some of us have larger thumbs than others) but it is surprising how quickly the art of producing an even pile is acquired.

Obviously it is wiser for a beginner to err on the side of making the loops slightly too long rather than too short as the pile can easily be cut shorter to the required length but not lengthened if the loops are made too short originally.

Slight trimming of the pile is always necessary and most people have favourite scissors for different types of needlework. Any good quality, sharp, medium-sized scissors do this trimming efficiently, but surgical scissors seem to be particularly good for the purpose. Workers generally develop their own pet action for trimming but personal experience suggests that an even pile is most easily produced if the rug is held level (i.e. on a horizontal plane) on the knees or table and the cut edge pushed away slightly from the pile already worked when evening it up.

The look of the pile is improved if it is "scrabbled" towards the worker with the finger nails after every few rows. This helps to remove the loose fluff of the wool from the surface of the rug and also encourages the cut ends of the wool to lie evenly. A comb does not do this as well as finger nails.

It will be noticed from the diagrams of both Surrey and Turkey stitches, that the strands of pile produced at the start and finish of the stitch are both pressed down by an "arm" across them when the knot is pulled tight. Each row of pile therefore tends to lie down towards the worker but, fortunately, they are held up by the pile already worked and merely lie back against this, making it all the easier to work the next row. Nevertheless, the pile as a whole does have a definite tendency to bend in one direction rather than any other when trodden upon and this explains the habit developed by loose mats or rugs on pile carpets to move or "walk" in the direction in which the pile of the carpet lies.

The rug having been started just inside the edging stitch, either close against it or one row in (see Chapter Five for further comments on this matter), it will be realized that there are several rows to be worked over the doubled-over canvas. This is naturally very tiresome, but there is no doubt that the doubled inch or so makes for strength and gives added weight at each end which encourages the rug to lie flat on the floor. When using single mesh canvas, the "double" is definitely difficult to work through accurately, but it can be done and has been done times without number, although by dealing with the edge by one of the methods suggested in Chapter Three it is avoided.

When the doubled part has been passed and the worker arrives at the single thickness of canvas a sigh of relief ensues, but a good job has been accomplished and the rough cut edge disappears into the pile to be seen no more.

As the pile rug grows it is necessary to double back most of the part already worked for convenient handling, and a long strong envelope inserted in the resulting fold of the rug between the piece being worked and that already done will prevent the current stitches from being sewn to the finished part of the rug (which will be underneath the envelope). Cardboard is not suitable for this purpose because flexibility is desirable.

Chapter Five

SMOOTH-FACED RUGS—
VARIETIES OF CROSS STITCH

SMOOTH-FACED rugs are started just inside the edging stitch, as are pile rugs, but with the unworked length of the canvas facing towards, instead away from, the worker.

Other differences as regards general treatment are that:

1. The turned-over cut edge should be on the underneath side of the rug instead of on the top. There is a school of thought that prefers to have the cut edge on top whatever type of rug is being made, but however neatly and strongly it is covered, this edge forms a ridge where the double canvas becomes single and therefore it is better to have it on the wrong side of the material for smooth-faced rugs.

2. When using pile stitches the starts and stops are all on the top of the rug. With flat stitches the new and old threads should be run in along the back of the work already completed. If attempts are made to do this on the front of the rug the resultant thickening invariably shows.

Avoid turning the canvas round. There is no incentive to do so when making a pile rug, but with flat stitches workers may feel a desire to experiment in this way and are warned most earnestly to resist such temptations as this practice is almost bound to lead to trouble and inaccuracies.

Cross stitch and its derivatives, already mentioned in Chapter Two, cannot be bettered for smooth-faced rugs. They are strong, cover the canvas well (owing to the fact that they all "slope" on the surface in the working, i.e. they all cross the warp and weft threads at an angle), and they produce attractive results particularly when they are combined with one another. They have also the advantage that they are very accommodating for certain types of design.

Cross Stitch

There can be very few people (women anyhow) who as children did not make a cross stitch mat for a Christmas present. Personally I have a vivid recollection of my first effort at embroidery at a kindergarten. This was a kettle holder in cross stitch worked in what I now realise to have been a peculiarly offensive combination of bright pink and green wool and which was received by my mother with tactful exclamations of gratitude and admiration.

Nearly everybody has a general knowledge of the working of cross stitch and realises that it is formed by two sloping stitches crossing one another at right angles and each covering one or more intersections of the canvas bars. In cross stitch embroidery there are two distinct methods of dealing with the stitch: (*a*) where a line of single sloping stitches is worked and then crossed by a similar line done in the reverse direction and (*b*) where each cross is completed before the next is made. This second method results in rather a firmer stitch and, generally speaking, covers the foundation material more efficiently than does method (*a*). As this matter of the complete covering of the canvas cannot be over-emphasised (it is so obviously one of the most important points in rug making) it is the counsel of perfection to employ method (*b*) wherever possible. Completing each stitch singly is, however, a tedious process where large expanses of one colour are to be worked, and in such cases method (*a*) can be used. If there is any doubt about the canvas being sufficiently covered it is a wise plan to lay a single length of wool over a double weft bar from left to right and then work the cross stitches over this in two stages according to method (*a*). This is one of the cases where personal initiative must take the place of hard and fast rules, bearing in mind that *no vestige of canvas foundation must be visible.*

Lines of cross stitch can be worked in several directions with great ease but it should be remembered that the top, i.e. the upper half, of the cross should always lie in the same direction throughout, e.g. from bottom left to top right. Any deviation from a regular slope of the top half spoils the general look of the rug and if variations of cross stitch are combined in one rug they should all have their top stitches sloping in the same direction, and bottom left to top right is generally found to be the most convenient for working.

Three ways of working the stitch are shown in Fig. 10A to D, each illustrating a different direction in which it can travel.

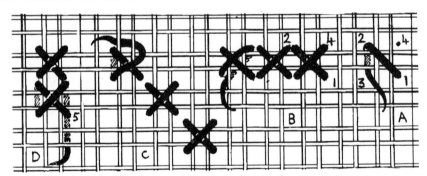

FIG. 10 *Working of cross stitch in different directions.*

It should be noted that:

(i) If the cross stitches are worked in a straight line from right to left there will be, on the back of the canvas, one short vertical and one short diagonal stitch, the order of entering the holes, alternately from the back and the front, being 1, 2, 3, 4 and then out again at 3 for the next stitch.

(ii) If the cross stitches are worked in a line diagonally upwards from right to left there will be, on the back of the canvas, one short vertical and one short horizontal stitch, the order of entering the holes being 1, 2, 3, 4 and then out again at 2 for the start of the next stitch.

(iii) If the cross stitches are worked in a downwards straight line there will be, on the back of the canvas, one short vertical and one long vertical stitch, the order of entering the holes being 1, 2, 3, 4, and down to 5 starting again from 5 for the next stitch.

In every case the stitch is completed before passing on to the next one and the top half of the cross slopes from bottom left to top right.

When two or more lengths of wool are used together care should be taken that these lie side by side on the top of the canvas and do not become twisted. As mentioned in connection with the edging stitch a half turn with the needle every two or three stitches helps to ensure this.

The best way of starting on a blank foundation is to hold the loose tail of the wool behind the canvas and work over it. When a small piece of the canvas has been covered it is easy to thread old and new tails along the back of the work.

The rug maker using flat stitches can never resist a sigh of regret for the perfection of the reverse side of a Surrey stitch rug, but he or she can be comforted by a glance at the back of many a "real" Oriental rug where neatness is *not* a strong point. Much can be done, however, to ensure a tidy appearance by running in the starting and finishing threads at the back on their own colours.

Long-legged Cross Stitch

This is similar to a flat version of the plaited edging stitch described in Chapter Two except that alternate parts of the stitch go on two and back one instead of on three and back two. Its close interlocking in the working ensures particularly good wearing qualities and at the same time it is very economical in wool. When used for a simple pattern it is rapid in execution and it can be very neat on the back—in fact if someone wishes to learn but one of the flat stitches, long-legged cross stitch is the one to master. It can be worked in straight lines from right to left, left to right, up or down (remembering to turn the direction of the stitch as desired rather than the canvas) and a judicious use of various directions can produce charming results. By working rows alternately backwards and forwards a ribbed effect is produced giving a particularly attractive texture.

In the previous chapter it was stated that many makers of pile rugs advocate the working of a row of long-legged cross stitch between the edging stitch and the start of the pile. There is no doubt that this helps to hold up the pile and increases its wearing qualities. If this long-legged row is used, it should be worked in the same colour as that of the edging stitch.

Some workers like a "platform" of a flat stitch or stitches and of anything from one to three or four inches deep at each end of a pile rug, and long-legged cross stitch is very suitable for this, possibly in combination with the next stitch to be described ("Rice stitch"). One of the advantages of the platform idea is that it can be used for working over the double canvas, and the pile begun when the single thickness has been reached. This plan is particularly helpful when using single mesh jute. When a flat stitched platform is to be large enough to cover all the doubled-over canvas, naturally the cut edge should be on the underside of the rug, as for one that is to be smooth-faced throughout. Whether the finished appearance of the rug looks as well as when the pile is taken up to within one row of the edge, or even to the edge itself, is purely a question of personal preference.

The start for long-legged as for the edging stitch is a plain cross stitch, the *lower half of which must be worked always in the direction in which the plait is to travel*, from right to left, left to right or up or down. Fig. 11A to D shows the start of the plait working from right to left and vice versa, and it will be noticed that at the back of the canvas the stitch is always vertical, not sometimes diagonal as in ordinary cross stitch.

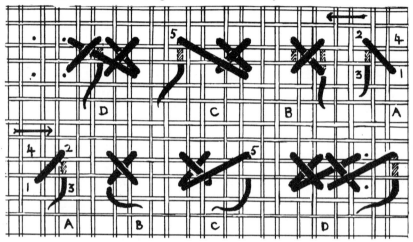

FIG. 11   *Working of long-legged cross stitch; top line from right to left, lower line from left to right.*

To finish a row the long forward stitch should be followed by the usual short stitch (the back one) and then by a short forward stitch instead of the usual long one, i.e. each row finishes with a cross stitch as well as starting with one. The same procedure applies to the finish of each colour block in a row when a pattern is being worked, thus ensuring the correct number of long stitches for each colour in turn. It will be noted from studying the diagrams how the plait develops from a simple cross stitch.

The best way to make a neat join when a new length of wool is needed is to end on the long ("on two") stitch and to run the remains of the old length in behind the work in the forward direction, preferably on the same colour. The "pull" on the wool tends to preserve the direction of slope of the last stitch. The new length should be run in along the back also and emerge at the front where it would have come out if continuing the plait. It is then in position for the short, backward stitch and the plait travels on as before with no visible join.

Wide Use of Long-legged Cross Stitch

One of the interests of embroidery lies in the numerous aliases of the stitches, and the alternative names Plaited Slav Stitch and Portuguese Cross Stitch show the wide range of long-legged cross stitch.

It is well worth while to track down Portuguese rugs in museums in order to see the delightful ways in which the stitch is used, and the interesting patterns evolved. Amusing animals play a large part in Portuguese rugs, adding much vitality to them, and possibly this aspect of their designs is due to the Portuguese character. Although I cannot claim more than a scant knowledge of the country and people, their general cheerfulness, sense of fun and love of brightness seem to be inherent in their embroideries and rugs as well as in other aspects of their daily life. Someone said to my husband and me: "We Portuguese are 'joyeux'", and certainly the truth of that epithet is borne out in the rugs over which we gloated. We also saw many evidences of fondness for animals, which trait may influence the introduction of so many live creatures into their designs. Fig. 12 shows motifs taken from various Portuguese rugs: the comic bird is very typical of the animals they introduce.

F I G. 12   *Motifs from Portuguese rugs.*

Rug makers who are lucky enough, as I was, to be able to visit Portugal will be charmed by the hand-made modern rugs, worked in the traditional stitch, and used casually in hotels and other public buildings, as well as in such surroundings as the Queluz Palace near Lisbon, part museum part palace, where State guests are accommodated and entertained. Many exquisite old rugs are to be seen in the rooms shown to the public, worked in long-legged cross stitch and generally in the traditionally predominant colours of blues and golds.

Even today in Portugal the Elizabethan chronicler's "good workman" visits the houses of his clients and works there until the carpet is completed. It is certainly an ideal arrangement that the design and colouring can be discussed daily with the householder and small alterations made if desired. It was an unforgettable incident when we entered the large, square hall of an hotel and saw there an obviously hand-made carpet that fitted into its surroundings perfectly. In reply to questions the answer was: "Oh, it was made for this hall", and the result was certainly enchanting, especially as an enormous log fire made the parquet floor and the big copper vessels set about the hall all glow, as well as showing up the wonderfully rich colourings of the carpet.

Rice Stitch

Rice stitch is the third of the cross stitch trio that offers so many possibilities to the rug maker. Why "Rice" stitch? Is it pictorial and do the small stitches that cross the four corners suggest rice grains, or was it called after an inventor named Rice? Of its other aliases "William and Mary" may conjure up pictures of the lonely queen finding solace in her canvas work and being attracted by this stitch which is now linked with her name, but "Cross-cornered cross stitch", an alternative frequently used, is purely descriptive, rather a mouthful and not very romantic.

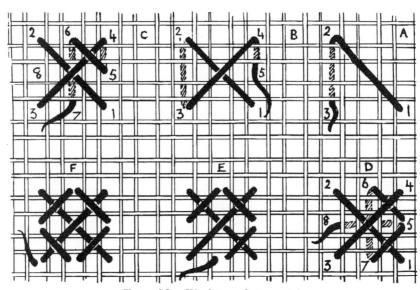

F I G. 13   *Working of rice stitch.*

As will be seen from Fig. 13A to F the foundation of rice stitch is a large cross, the arms of which are twice the size of a simple cross stitch. When this has been worked each of its four corners is crossed in turn by a small diagonal stitch and the final result is an attractive rosette with a slightly raised centre. This latter is due to the corners of the big cross being held down. As the diagrams show, the stitch is worked in six stages in such a way that the needle invariably makes a horizontal or vertical (never a diagonal) stitch on the back, thus ensuring that the back is as neat as possible. The following is the order of working:

From hole 1 to hole 2 and down to hole 3.
From hole 3 to hole 4 and down to hole 5.
From hole 5 to hole 6 and down to hole 7.
From hole 7 to hole 5 and across to hole 8.
From hole 8 up to hole 6 and down to hole 7.
From hole 7 up to hole 8 and down to hole 3.

The needle is then in position to work the next large cross. It will be observed that the wool goes from hole 6 to hole 7 for *two* of the long stitches.

The stitch is very strong but it is extravagant as regards the amount of wool used. It will be found, also, that when a number of rows of rice stitch have been worked one after the other it is necessary to insert "back stitches" between each row of these or the canvas is inclined to show through.

Back Stitch

This has the appearance of a continuous line of stitches like the seam made by a sewing machine. It can be worked along any line of holes on the canvas, whether in weft or warp directions or diagonally. To start a line for example between two rows of rice stitches, the needle point is brought up from behind the work through the second hole in the line and taken back and down through the first (or end) hole. It is then brought up through the third hole, back and down through the second and so on, i.e. alternately on two holes underneath the work and back one hole on the upper side till the line is finished. It will be noticed that all the stitches on the upper side of the work are the short ones made in the backward direction (i.e. opposite to that in which the line of stitches is proceeding), hence the name of the stitch. With double mesh canvas the "holes" referred to will be the large ones bounded by double bar wefts and warps.

The need for back stitches can be obviated if rice stitch is used in conjunction with ordinary and long-legged cross stitches. The three work in very well together since one row of rice stitch equals two of either of the others in depth. The texture of a rug wherein all three are used can be very pleasing. As both rice and long-legged cross stitch are heavy stitches, i.e. give a rather thick covering to the canvas, it is advisable to reinforce the simple cross stitches when only a few of these are used with the other two so that they match them in weight. This is managed by doubling the lower half of the cross stitch *after* the whole stitch has been completed, being careful to pass the needle underneath the upper half.

The use of these three varieties of cross stitch in one rug is shown in Fig. 14—part of a landing floor covering. The strip photographed is the small, top-of-the-stairs piece, measuring 2 feet 3 inches by 4 feet 3 inches, the main strip being 2 feet 3 inches wide and 28 feet long. The latter was worked in one piece, on 4s canvas, and the colours, deep blues and reds, with greens of a slightly lighter tone, were chosen for their dirt-resisting qualities. The carpet has "worn clean" and after ten years has shown no signs of wear except at the entrance to the most-used bedroom, where the edging needed slight repair after nine years. It took four years to make, working only in the evenings after eight o'clock—and *not* going to bed at "all hours". The narrow strip or line seen on the photograph to divide the border pattern from the "field" (i.e. the main part of the carpet), is worked in "deep"

FIG. 14 *Strip of landing carpet worked in rice
stitch, cross stitch and long-legged cross stitch on 4s
canvas. Designed by G. V. Mathews and worked by
Sibyl I. Mathews. Chiefly blues with dull greens and
reds. Size 27 × 51 inches.*

long-legged cross stitch and along the carpet instead of across it. This variety of long-legged cross stitch is worked over two double bars instead of one, thus doubling the width of the area covered by the row of stitches (Fig. 15A to D). Such a change of direction of working and slight variation of the stitch itself can be extremely useful in adding an interesting contrast to the general texture of a rug.

The dark square patches are worked in rice stitch.

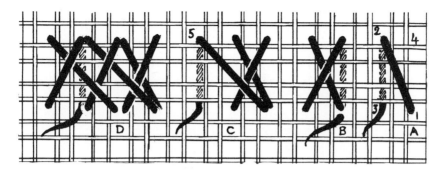

FIG. 15 *Working of deep, long-legged cross stitch.*

An enlarged version of the Persian "trees" forming the border is shown in Fig. 16 where the effect of the regular rib can be noted and also the final stitch which finishes each colour block in turn, and the deep, long-legged cross stitch at right angles to the main design.

When the carpet was made many years ago I had not realised the supreme importance of outlining the pattern (see Chapter Seven). Luckily the carpet looks well in the position for which it was made but there is no doubt that correct outlining would have improved its appearance.

FIG. 16 *Detail of carpet shown in Fig. 14.*

Tent Stitch or Petit Point

Before the general advent of pile rugs and carpets to England in the late eighteenth century many embroidered ones were made, a great many of them in cross stitch, some in long-legged cross stitch but possibly even more in "Tent stitch", another name for which is Petit Point. Many of these were of very fine workmanship and would be used as "table carpets", but rugs so made are extremely satisfactory as floor coverings.

Each stitch is completed with a single motion of the needle and its finished appearance is that of the top half of an ordinary cross stitch, sloping across an intersection of the canvas threads. All the stitches on the front slope the same way, viz, from bottom left to top right. For reasons to be mentioned below tent stitch should be worked along diagonal lines where the design allows, following directions alternately downwards from left to right and upwards from right to left. When working along a downwards diagonal line, each stitch is made with the needle facing straight towards the worker, and when working upwards, it is made with the needle facing sideways in a straight line from right to left. In both cases as Figs. 19 and 21 show (for double mesh canvas) the needle is taken *over* an intersection of two double bars of the canvas and either horizontally or vertically *under* two double bars (according to the direction of working).

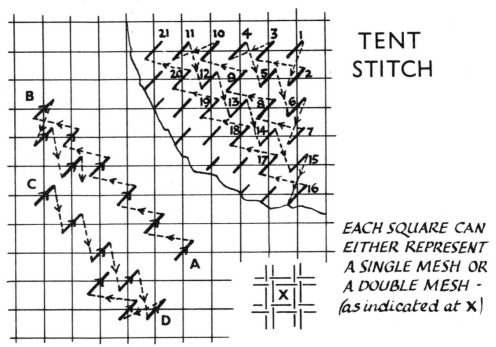

FIG. 17   *Tent stitch. Dotted lines represent paths taken by the needle across the* back *of the canvas. Numbers in the top right corner give the order in which stitches are made on the face of the canvas. They refer to stitches and not to squares.*

When the stitch is worked in the above manner the back of the canvas becomes closely covered with a basket weave which is both strong and of pleasant appearance. This is the main reason for working along diagonal lines rather than in horizontal straight lines, but in addition this procedure has been found by many workers to reduce the tendency of the rug to get out of shape.

The majority of people find it perfectly easy to work up and down diagonal lines but encounter difficulties when it comes to working the stitch to cover a rectangular area. The problem is how to turn the stitch when it meets a straight edge.

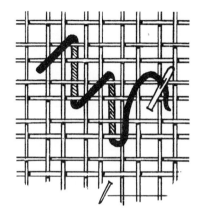

FIG. 18 *The turn at the bottom of the downward line preparatory to going upwards.*

FIG. 19 *The needle, having made the turn, starting horizontally for the second line (upwards).*

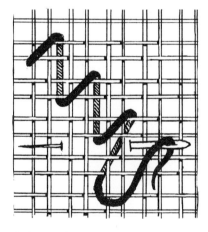

Fig. 17 shows a corner of such an area fully worked and the order in which the stitches should be made. The stitches at the top of the diagonal lines form the top horizontal straight edge and those at the bottom form the right-hand vertical straight edge. Figs. 18 and 19 show in detail how the turn should be worked at the bottom of a downward line preparatory to going upwards and Figs. 20 and 21 at the top of an upward line preparatory to going downwards. It will be seen that the first stitch of the upward line comes vertically below the last stitch of the downward line at the side edge, while the first stitch of a downward line comes horizontally to the left of the last stitch of an upward line at the top edge. Fig. 17 indicates at B and D how the lines would be turned at the left hand vertical edge and at the bottom horizontal edge of a rectangular area. Figs. 20 and 21 are overleaf.

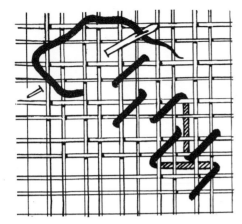

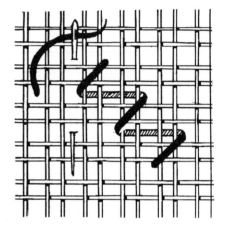

FIG. 20 *The needle, having gone down and up, making the turn at the top for the third line of stitches (down).*

FIG. 21 *The needle, having made the turn, going downwards again.*

Special features of the stitch are:

(*a*) No parts of the stitch cross on the face of the canvas so that a peculiarly smooth and flat surface results. This ensures good wearing qualities since friction is evenly distributed.

(*b*) In a fully worked area of tent stitch, no hole in the canvas is threaded by the wool more than twice, in which respect it differs from all the other flat stitches considered in this chapter. This feature enables an exceptionally fine mesh of canvas to be used for a given amount of wool in the needle without the holes being overcrowded. Conversely it enables an exceptionally thick wool to be used with a given canvas. The above facts are of importance when matching wool thickness and canvas—see Chapter Two, page 20.

(*c*) As previously stated, for single mesh canvas satisfactory results are only obtained with most stitches if a *pair* of successive canvas threads is treated as one double bar of double mesh canvas. With tent stitch, on the other hand, the best results are obtained when *each* canvas thread is treated as a double bar of double mesh canvas. Thus, a single mesh canvas with 8 threads to the inch is equivalent to 8s in double mesh canvas when tent stitch is used but only to 4s when most other stitches are used. This is of great importance when a design is to be worked requiring a fine mesh canvas.

(*d*) A useful feature of tent stitch for certain designs is that the unfinished edge of an area being worked along diagonal lines always presents a "toothed" appearance. The "teeth" are, in fact, projecting half-stitches which will ultimately interleave with similar half stitches in the continuation of the work. Consequently if the colours of the original and continued work are different, the interleaving will produce the effect of an intermediate colour, i.e. of "shading" from one colour into the other. This special feature of tent stitch is most useful when large surfaces of background need to be "broken" by variations of shade, or several shades of a colour in a small area are required as for representing, say, a flower.

(*e*) Lastly the smooth surface of tent stitch, in addition to making for hard wear, is especially adapted for showing up an intricate pattern, though on the other hand, this smoothness adds to the monotony of patternless areas. Hence one of the advantages of the shading possibilities with this stitch.

Rugs made in tent stitch can be very lovely, and on the whole (though it is unwise to generalise) they are more satisfying when worked throughout in the one stitch than when it is combined with others. This statement is not, of course, to be taken as applying to canvas work in general, as distinct from rugs, and is inevitably to some extent a matter of personal taste. If a combination of stitches is preferred it is best to use single mesh canvas (10 or 8 stitches to the inch) when the tent stitch will be worked on an intersection of 2 threads, and other stitches, e.g. cross stitch or long-legged, over two pairs of threads (equal to 1 double bar).

It is almost a *sine qua non* that tent stitch rugs should be made on rather fine canvas if the stitch is to be seen at its best. In double mesh canvas a 7s canvas is a good medium size for a rug that will not absorb too much time but, in general, the finer the canvas (within reason) the more beautiful should be the rug. This is particularly true when floral patterns are used as these are bound to involve curves and the greater the number of stitches per square inch the more nearly the effect of a curve can be approached.

The rug illustrated at Fig. 22 was worked on 10s canvas and is an excellent example of the effect that results from using a fine foundation. The curves flow and the whole design has an elegance that could not have been produced on coarse canvas. At the time this book went to press, Mr Thesiger had nearly finished another carpet on similar canvas which he had designed for an overall size of about 12 feet square, entailing the working of well over 2 million stitches. Such a monumental carpet should be an inspiration to rug enthusiasts as an example of what may be accomplished.

Some workers like to use a double mesh canvas for their work and to produce, over a limited area, the effect of a canvas of twice as fine a mesh (i.e. permitting four times as many stitches per square inch) by forcing apart or "splitting" the double bars and treating the result as single mesh. This scheme is not advised except for experienced workers who wish to produce fine pictures within coarser frames.

With most workers a rug made in tent stitch is particularly liable to get out of shape and it is safest to have it mounted on a frame for working. Mr Tattersall speaks of a wonderful table carpet worked in tent stitch with silk, measuring 13 feet by 5 feet 9 inches and with 400 stitches to the square inch, dated 1600. Unfortunately the carpet had been pulled very much out of the square and in order that this should not be too obvious it was exhibited

FIG. 22   *Rug in tent stitch on 10s canvas, designed and worked by Mr Ernest Thesiger. Main colouring a variety of blues and golds. Size 8 feet 8 inches × 5 feet 8 inches.*

FIG. 23 *Rug in tent stitch, on 7s canvas designed and worked in Mr Pontremoli's workrooms. Variety of natural flower colourings on light background. Size 8 feet 8 inches × 6 feet 9 inches.*

on a table that was equally irregular. Of course where a frame is used this type of rug is not so comfortable to make as other flat stitched varieties—sitting at a frame does not mean such relaxation as does the arm-chair after a day's work. Tent stitch is, however, a popular one and many rugs have been worked in it entirely without the use of a frame and successfully stretched back into shape, as necessary, after completion. Of course an expert worker may be able to make a tent stitch rug, without a frame, that will not need this stretching.

It is of special interest to note that the late Queen Mary used this stitch for all her rugs and for her famous carpet.

Up to a few years ago tent stitch rugs and carpets were hand-made as a commercial proposition in the workrooms of the late Mr Pontremoli at Spring Street, W.2, (where repairing of carpets is still carried out by skilled craftsmen). He employed many girls and, although the finished articles were naturally very costly, their beauty was such that he did not lack orders and it was the gradual dearth of new workers that eventually killed the industry—a sad story similar to the end of the hand-knotted carpets at Wilton. The work was done on frames, many embroiderers sitting in front of one of these in a long row when the carpet being made was a large one, and a strong linen canvas was used (with double warp and single weft threads) giving about 6½ stitches to the inch, and both canvas and wool were especially produced for Mr Pontremoli's use.

Many rugs and carpets were made at Spring Street for individual orders, including two for Princess Alexandra and the Duke of Kent when they were children, but among all that came from the Pontremoli workrooms none can surpass in interest the Hunting Carpet. This is a magnificent *tour de force* as regards its conception, artistry and technical workmanship. Mr Pontremoli loved the English countryside and scene, and everything connected with a hunt is embodied in the carpet. Much fine work (when the warp threads of his special canvas were split so as greatly to increase the usual number of stitches per square inch) goes to form the figures, the hounds and such realistic details as the hunt "Cap" with the coins falling into it.

The border shows the hounds in full cry across fields, with many groups of trees and above them clouds floating in a blue sky—but not too blue for an English winter. The colouring is faithful and the wools used by Mr Pontremoli's workers included so many shades of every colour that the whole scene could be reproduced with most careful attention to detail.

The detailed design for the carpet was carried out by an artist following Mr Pontremoli's general concept and under his guidance. The carpet is of an imposing size, measuring 27 feet 6 inches by 14 feet 6 inches (too large to be satisfactorily illustrated in this book). The drawing-room in Mr Pontremoli's house was of a size to show the carpet to its full advantage and he and his wife used to derive much pleasure from studying its details.

I am greatly indebted to Mrs Pontremoli for being allowed to write about her lovely possession and also for permission to use one of the Pontremoli rugs as an illustration of the possibilities of tent stitch (Fig. 23).

Chapter Six

SMOOTH-FACED RUGS—
SOME UNUSUAL STITCHES

ENTHUSIASTIC rug makers are bound to be experimentalists, and, apart from the cross stitch group, many and varied flat stitches can be tried. There is a slight tendency among embroiderers who wish to make rugs to think that all canvas work stitches are also suitable for rugs, but this is not the case. Once again it must be emphasised that hard-wearing qualities are the first consideration in the selection of the stitches. Experience has proved that the most satisfactory stitches to use are those which either interlock (e.g. long-legged) or are tied down in the working such as rice stitch, or cover the canvas in a sloping direction such as tent stitch. Some of them possess two of these properties which makes them particularly serviceable.

French Stitch

French Stitch belongs to the "tied down" category and although it may seem somewhat elaborate at first sight it is not any more so in reality than rice stitch, to which it bears a distinct relationship. Its completed shape is a rosette (see Fig. 24) and is such that succes-sive stitches will only pack closely together if they are worked along diagonal lines. There-fore certain types of design suit it better than others.

French stitch is one that does not combine very well with others owing to its invariable diagonal direction of progression, but it is a most intriguing stitch to work. An attractive effect results if it is used for the field of a rug, framed in long-legged cross stitch, with the border worked in a combination of long-legged and rice stitch. Fig. 25 shows a simple all-over pattern where this plan is used. The enlarged corner of it (Fig. 26) shows how, where the diagonal meets the long-legged framework, half stitches have to be inserted between the alternate complete rosettes in order to make the continuous top row, while at the sides two little straight stitches (the ends of the long bars) appear between the finished rosettes. It should be noted that a single row of complete rosettes outlines each block of pattern.

The figures and numbers will repay careful study before trying out the stitch. It will then be realised that it consists of two horizontal bars laid between the same two holes, viz. 1 and 2, each of which is tied down in turn by a short vertical stitch. It can be worked in any of four diagonal directions depending upon which of these is the most convenient:

A. Downwards from left to right.
B. Downwards from right to left.

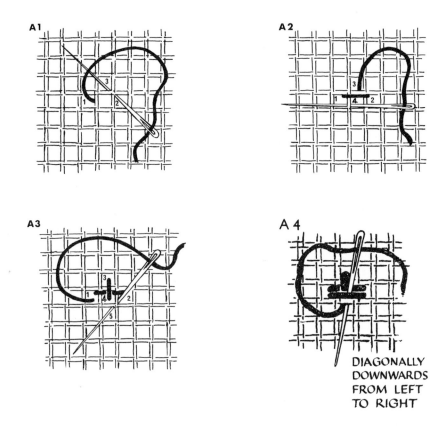

FIG. 24　*A1–A4. French stitch worked downwards from left to right.*

C.　Upwards from left to right.
D.　Upwards from right to left.

For A the needle is brought out at hole 1, taken across to hole 2 and up diagonally behind the canvas to emerge at hole 3. Then the resulting long bar is tied down by going over it into hole 4 and returning to hole 1. The process is repeated from hole 1 to hole 2 but the needle is then taken *down* diagonally to hole 5 and the second (lower) bar is tied down by going over it into hole 4 between the two bars and out again at hole 5. It will thus be seen that there are four distinct movements for each stitch and Fig. 24 A1 to A4 illustrate this clearly.

A rosette will now have been made and the line of these can proceed downwards to the right. In the next stitch hole 5 (where the first rosette finished) takes the place of hole 1, and hole 2 of hole 3.

When working downwards from right to left (B) the stitch is worked exactly as described for A except that after the final tie down in A4 the needle is brought out two holes to the left of hole 5 for the start of the next stitch.

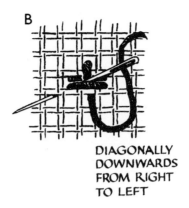

DIAGONALLY
DOWNWARDS
FROM RIGHT
TO LEFT

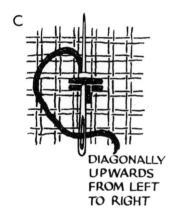

DIAGONALLY
UPWARDS
FROM LEFT
TO RIGHT

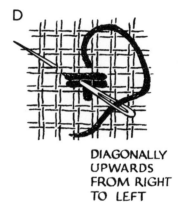

DIAGONALLY
UPWARDS
FROM RIGHT
TO LEFT

FIG. 24   *B, C, D. French stitch worked in other directions.*

When travelling upwards the order of the tying down of the long bars is reversed, the lower bar being tied down first. Thus:

Up from left to right, Fig. 24 C.

The needle is brought out at hole 1, taken across to hole 2 and *down* diagonally behind the canvas to emerge at hole 5. Then the resulting long bar is tied down by going over it into hole 4 and returning behind to hole 1. The process is repeated from hole 1 to hole 2 but the needle is then taken *up* diagonally to hole 3 and the second (top) bar tied down by going over it into hole 4 between the two horizontal bars and again out at hole 3. For the next stitch, to travel upwards from left to right, hole 3 takes the place of hole 1 and hole 2 of hole 5.

Up from right to left. Fig. 24 D.

The process is similar to the above except that after the top bar has been tied down the needle emerges two holes to the left of hole 3 after going into hole 4 instead of going straight up again to hole 3.

Again—the work should never be turned. If some of the rosettes are made sideways to each other the whole effect of the stitch would be spoilt.

FIG. 26 *Detail of French stitch rug.*

(Detailed caption on opposite page).

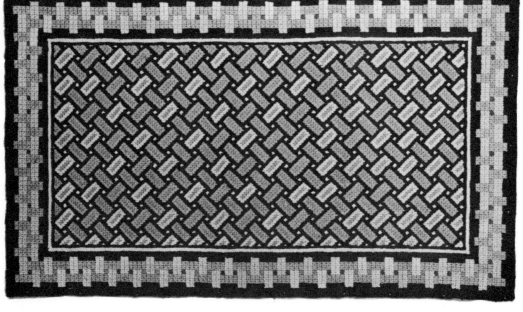

FIG. 25 *French stitch rug.*

On opposite page:

FIG. 25 *French stitch rug on 5s canvas, worked by Mrs Lewis from a design supplied by Dr Sibyl Welsh. Red outlines, fawns and greens for fillings. Size 26 × 45 inches.*

FIG. 26 *Enlarged corner of French stitch rug (a slightly different version of 25).*

Soumak Stitch

Soumak Stitch is one of the most fascinating of all the stitches recommended for smooth-faced rugs; in fact people who are once enthralled by it can seldom be persuaded to use anything else. It belongs to the interlocking group, and rugs made by this method seem to wear indefinitely. One of the first known exponents of the stitch made five exquisite Soumak rugs in crewel wool on 10s canvas two of which are known to have endured extremely hard wear for over twenty years without showing any signs of such use.[1] Probably the reason for this is largely because, apart from the close interlocking, the surface of rugs made in this way is particularly smooth with correspondingly even distribution of friction.

When worked, this stitch is similar in appearance to stocking stitch in knitting, and there is a version of it that is actually called Knitting stitch. This, however, takes two rows to produce the surface effect that Soumak stitch does in one row, and moreover does not interlock. A special feature of Soumak stitch is that each completed stitch finishes at the hole where it started, thus enabling the worker to travel easily in several directions and so work patterns in the most convenient way. It is often a great help, especially when working a fine rug, to be able to put in the outline of an elaborate motif first and then fill it in, and this is especially simple to do when using Soumak stitch.

Rugs worked by this method bear a close resemblance to the real eastern Soumak rugs woven on a loom. The name is said to be derived from Shemakha, a town in the province of Shirvan near Baku, and the rugs have many of the characteristics of the Caucasian group as a whole. Their designs are nearly always mainly geometrical, the field of the rugs consisting frequently of large medallions with very stylised flowers and fruit as subsidiary ornamentation and many hooks and sharp angles.

When working this stitch the canvas should be held at right angles to the position used for every other stitch hitherto discussed, i.e. with the unworked length of canvas to the left of the worker and the selvedges running sideways across the knees. In whichever direction the stitches travel, the V which each stitch makes should have its sharp point facing towards the worker. The resemblance to Soumak weaving is lost if the stitch is incorrectly worked so that the V made by each stitch points along the warp of the canvas instead of along the weft as it should do.

---

[1] It may be mentioned that domestic animals were regularly given their food upon these beautiful rugs without even a newspaper between the rugs and the animals' dishes.

Method of Working

1. Each stitch is begun between the two threads of a canvas weft double bar (i.e. splitting the bar) at hole 1. The needle is then taken up *over* two warp double bars into hole 2, *under* a weft double bar of two threads from right to left into hole 3, returns to the original starting point at hole 1 and, if a straight line downwards is required, drops down between the threads of the next weft double bar to hole 4. The stitch is then repeated exactly as before. Fig. 27A shows this process in complete detail.

SELVEDGE EDGE   SELVEDGE EDGE

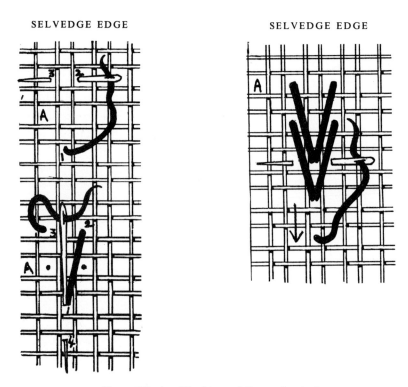

FIG. 27 *A   Working of Soumak stitch.*

2. Should the worker wish to proceed in a straight line from right to left, the needle is inserted between the double weft bar to the *left* of the finished stitch instead of dropping down, see Fig. 27B.

3. For a diagonal line downwards from right to left, the needle drops *down* one bar diagonally each time, see Fig. 27C.

4. For a diagonal line upwards from right to left, the needle moves *up* one bar diagonally, see Fig. 27D.

In all four cases it must be remembered that *each single stitch in turn* must be worked and completed according to the directions for 1 (above), i.e. from hole 1, via 2 and 3 and back to 1, continuing then in the direction required as shown in the Figures.

SELVEDGE EDGE

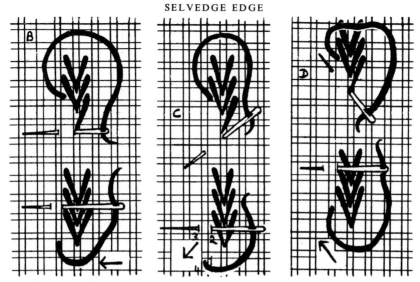

FIG. 27 *B–D Working of Soumak stitch in different directions.*

Pitfalls and Hints

1. The stitch is incredibly easy to work when once the basic method has been mastered, but some people find difficulty in remembering that it is always the *weft* double bars (which run straight towards the worker when the canvas is held in the correct position for this stitch) that are split. The fact that there are two threads in each warp double bar in the canvas must be forgotten when working the stitch, and if workers find any temptation to put their needle between these the remedy is to bind them together with thread and make them into one until the working of the stitch becomes mechanical. It is this continual splitting of the weft bars that makes it far easier to use double rather than single mesh canvas for Soumak stitch. The count of the stitch can be very irritating with single mesh wherein two successive equidistant threads have to be treated as a single weft or warp double bar.

2. *Direction.* It is, of course, possible to work straight upwards; from left to right in straight lines; diagonally down from left to right; diagonally up from left to right; in fact in the four opposite directions to those suggested and shown on the diagrams. The reason for not recommending these directions is that the action for their working is clumsy, being somewhat back-handed, but it is sometimes useful to work in these ways even if awkward. It is however advisable to become thoroughly proficient first with the four easier methods of travelling. On the other hand for a left-handed worker these would be the most natural directions to use.

3. *Outlines and Filling In.* It is a good plan to experiment with the outlines of a small pattern and its filling in before embarking upon a complete rug so as to see how the stitches fit in with each other. When filling in it is easy to omit occasional stitches if care is not exercised.

4. *Designing for a Soumak Rug.* It must be remembered always that each stitch is worked

over two warp bars of the canvas, so that in designing a rug on squared paper for Soumak stitch the number of squares used in the width must be one less than the number of bars between the selvedges of the canvas, e.g. if the canvas has 135 bars in its width there must be only 134 squares (i.e. stitches) shown on the paper.

5. *Importance of Accuracy*. It is not easy to rectify mistakes when making Soumak rugs as the stitches are so closely interlocked that unpicking is difficult; therefore complete accuracy in working is essential. As mentioned before, it is partly this interlocking that ensures the long-wearing qualities of these rugs, while at the same time they are economical in wool and correspondingly light in weight.

6. *Back Stitch Finish*. Where the stitch meets the selvedges it is necessary to work a row of back stitches between the Vs and the edging stitch when the rug is finished, otherwise a gap is left which shows the canvas and spoils the final appearance of the rug.

7. *Working through the "double" canvas* at the cut ends is particularly tiresome in this stitch and when very fine canvas is used doubling over can be avoided by machining several times along the last two or three rows of the canvas, then machining a length of narrow binding over this rough edge and finally working the edging stitch over this. When this method of finishing the edges is adopted the corners may show a slight tendency to curl, in which case it is advisable to attach rubber angle pieces at each corner. These can be obtained in varying sizes from good furnishers. An alternative plan is to work long-legged cross stitch over an inch of "double" at the end of the rug and then to start on the Soumak stitch. This results in a firmer edge but does not look so well.

8. *Tension of Stitch*. Finally, of all stitches Soumak needs most care as regards the tension applied to the wool. This should never be more than the minimum necessary to pull the wool through the canvas, and the thickness of the wool in the needle should not exceed what allows it to pass easily between the split weft bars. The Red Soumak (Fig. 30) developed a waist-line in working (which luckily disappeared after stretching) and this was probably because some of the wool used was thicker than it should have been.

Interlocking Gobelin Stitch

This is undoubtedly the easiest to work of all reliable rug stitches and is a boon to those who wish to make a rug rapidly and without much in the way of design. It is worked backwards and forwards in horizontal rows from selvedge to selvedge which means that it is ideal for a striped rug and it can also be used as a quick stitch with which to cover a platform, as suggested in Chapter Five, before the main design of a rug is started.

The stitch is the first half of a cross stitch worked over one double bar horizontally but two vertically, see Fig. 28.

At the end of each row the last stitch drops down an extra hole at the back of the canvas and then the stitch travels back in the opposite direction in exactly the same way, so that the first row of stitches will be crossed in their bottom halves. It is necessary to finish the first stitch of the first row and the last stitch of the final row with the other (short) half of a cross stitch in order to cover the canvas completely. The illustration Fig. 29 shows a rug made entirely in this stitch.

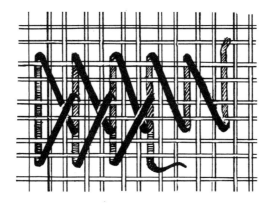

FIG. 28   *Working of Interlocking Gobelin stitch.*

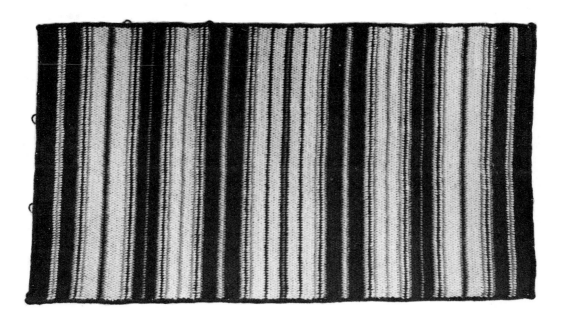

FIG. 29   *Striped rug in Interlocking Gobelin stitch, designed and worked by Mrs Horton. Grey, blue and cherry red.   Size 27 × 48 inches.*

FIG. 30 *Red Soumak stitch rug on 10s canvas, designed by*
G. V. Mathews and worked by Sibyl I. Mathews.   Size
32 × 65 inches.

Chapter Seven

DESIGN AND COLOUR—GENERAL PRINCIPLES

ASSUMING correct technique the main criterion for assessing the quality of a rug is its design and colouring, and it is questionable which of these is the cart and which the horse —they are both of such supreme importance.

The majority of people will wish to blend varying quantities of colours, or possibly several shades of two or three colours, with the main colour of their rugs, and it is easier to work out the proportions of these satisfactorily if the design is planned first, at any rate in broad outline.

Design

That designing a rug is considered by many to be a formidable task is proved by the fact that ready stencilled canvas and printed charts must be sold by the thousand, judging by the way in which exactly the same rug appears again and again at craft exhibitions. This is not only extremely dull, it is also unnecessary, because there is no possible doubt that the majority of rug makers who show these uninteresting specimens could, with a little trouble, produce rugs that would express their own individuality and give that sense of achievement not to be obtained by pure copying. In other words they could create a rug instead of merely working one.

Obviously the trained designer, who is also an artist as regards line and colour, starts with an enormous advantage which puts her or him in a category far removed from the majority of those for whom it is hoped that these suggestions will be helpful. But even so the most important point for rug makers to bear in mind is that *it is not essential to be able to draw in order to design a first-class rug.* What is vital is:

(*a*) To have so much enthusiasm for the craft that all possible sources of inspiration and help as regards design and colour are considered and sought after and (*b*) not to fear simplicity. A plain, striped rug can show initiative and will be far more worth while in its accomplishment than an elaborate rug, however technically perfect, a replica of which is likely to be seen any day in a neighbour's house.

Some Guiding Principles in Design

When thinking of rug designs it is advisable and helpful to start by considering the ways in which rugs are used and seen in the Western world:

69

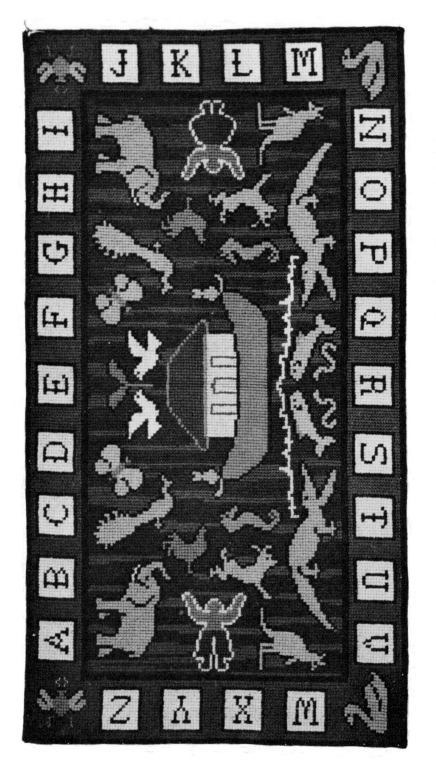

FIG. 31 "Noah's Ark" on 5s canvas, worked by G. V. Mathews from a "co-operative" design. Cross stitch with long-legged cross stitch background. Blues, golds, off-white, red. Size 27 × 48 inches

1. A rug is usually placed on the floor and is meant to be walked on.
2. It is seen from varying distances.
3. It may be looked at from several directions.

These points have as their corollary the facts that a rug design should be basically conventional, bold and (largely) symmetrical—although the desirability of the latter is partly a matter of personal opinion as is so much else to do with rug making.

1. Apart from considerations of suitability, the majority of people do not wish to walk upon a cottage practically covering a rug, a bunch of colossal roses or two fat pink mermaids on a sea-shore, all of which have actually been seen at exhibitions, and generally speaking the use of simple geometrical forms is far preferable. There are, of course, moments when the urge to "break out" is ungovernable (witness the Dragon) but it is wiser on the whole to curb the imagination and consider whether a rug designed in the nature of a jest will be one the worker will wish to live with for a lifetime and hand on to the next generation.

All naturalistic objects should be used with great care, especially in designs to be worked on coarse canvas for a general purposes rug, where they cannot be recommended. In the case of a really large carpet, such as the Pontremoli Hunting Carpet (Chapter Five) much can be introduced that would be out of place in an ordinary sized rug—and it must be remembered that many of its fascinating details are worked in stitches of over 100 to the square inch, this being made possible by splitting the double bars of the canvas.

The Alphabet-cum-Noah's Ark rug (Fig. 31) was designed and made especially for a child, to be used solely as a nursery rug and probably to be crawled on and sat on rather than walked on.

Its designing entailed a considerable amount of argument. An ark at each end of the rug would have resulted in a better design than one in the centre which was upside down when looked at from one direction, but no child would "stand" for two arks, so one it had to be. An attempt to induce the animals to walk "two by two" was unsatisfactory so the plan was reluctantly changed to including two animals of each kind arranged symmetrically but *not* side by side. When the design was completed and the border actually begun it was remembered (literally in the watches of the night) that there was no kangaroo and that error had to be hastily rectified. It was thought that the border would be better without animals except in the corners and anyhow a firm great-aunt decided that amusement must be coupled with instruction.

2. Although the Caliph in the *Arabian Nights* sat on a glittering throne covered with seven carpets, people in the East generally sit on the floor so that their carpets are near their eye level, and this probably accounts for the great importance and beauty of the detail in the best Oriental rugs and carpets.

In the West a rug's position on the floor means that it is usually seen from varying distances so that it is obviously wise that the main pattern should be bold (which does *not* mean vast in size) in order that it should be effective, and individual originality and initiative can be used for detail within the main framework of the design.

The Farmyard rug (Fig. 2) illustrates this point. The three medallions form the basic, seen-at-a-glance design and the animals and small geometric motifs are the broken background detail, no one motif being particularly in evidence. (See page 10.)

When considering the use of this background detail in needle-made rugs it is important to realise the limitations imposed by the foundation material. The canvas is composed of squares and it is only when these are small that the lines of knots or flat stitches can appear to flow as a curve instead of being an angular progression. From this it will be seen that designs embodying curves should only be used on fine rugs and that the more holes to the inch there are on the canvas the more interesting and intricate can be the detail. The pile rug illustrated in Fig. 32 shows, in the water-lilies, how the effect of a curve can be produced on 8s canvas. The design is taken from a Chinese bowl. The maker of this rug considers that the general balance of the design would have been improved, and the lilies would have shown to greater advantage, if they had been placed a little farther from the end borders.

Fig. 32 *"Water-lily" rug in Turkey or Ghiordes knot on 8s canvas. Worked by Mrs Elston; design adapted by her from a Chinese bowl. Green background with red-pink, blue and yellow. Size 26 × 45 inches.*

As a further illustration of an important effect of the size of canvas used the reader is referred to the pony in the bottom left-hand medallion of the Forest rug, Fig. 33. The number of stitches used is 24 in the length and 16 in the height and it would be difficult to make the animal look like a pony if there were fewer stitches.

On the 10s canvas used the pony measures $2\frac{1}{2}$ inches by $1\frac{1}{2}$ inches.

On 5s canvas it would measure 5 inches by 3 inches.

On 3s canvas it would measure 8 inches by 5 inches.

Broadly speaking, therefore, animals and figures should only be used when making fine rugs where they are intended to form part of the detail. On the Red Soumak, Fig. 28 (10s canvas) the "worms" which straggle sinuously across its background are effective but they would look clumsy on 5s and worse on 3s.

Curves come more naturally with tent stitch than with any other stitch owing to its nature (see Chapter Five, page 52). With this stitch, therefore, greater latitude is permissible in types of design, but even so the finer the canvas the more flowing the curves. For the majority of rugs nothing coarser than 7s is really satisfactory for a design that is not basically geometric.

3. As rugs on the floor may be approached and seen from several directions the main pattern and the details enhancing it should be so arranged that they look well from whatever angle the rug is regarded. This again makes the geometrical pattern the easiest to deal with, and if any figures, animals or other realistic objects are introduced it is advisable that when seen from any direction some at least of them should be upright. The Forest rug, the Farmyard rug and the Noah's Ark rug all illustrate this point. The great exceptions to this are the Eastern prayer rugs, which are planned deliberately so that they should be seen to best advantage when used for their avowed object.

Rugs of Unusual Shapes

It is important to be able to move rugs so as to alter the focus of wear, and this emphasises the fact that it is better to make rectangular rugs, which look well anywhere, rather than to attempt odd shapes such as half-moons. With these peculiar shaped rugs (*a*) a great deal of canvas is cut to waste, (*b*) it is impossible to work an edging stitch on them satisfactorily —little spikes of canvas are bound to show through, (*c*) they can be used in one position only, and (*d*) it is extremely difficult to work out anything in the way of a satisfactory design which can fulfil its function of being decoratively pleasing, since the discipline of counted threads does not lend itself to such a shape.

Sources of Design

Nothing will be so practically useful as well as infinitely rewarding artistically as the study of good Eastern rugs and carpets. Luckily there are many places where these can now be seen as, apart from well arranged museums, there are almost invariably many such rugs on view in the old historic houses now open to the public. Naturally it is far easier to gain help and inspiration if a rug can be handled, and if such permission is given it is generally quite possible to count the stitches on the back if not the front, and in this way many patterns can be extracted and built up to form individual designs.

A small book of squared paper should be a "must" in every rug maker's pocket or handbag. It is invaluable to be able to jot down ideas for future use, however roughly these may be drawn. Among many sketches made in such a way and used in this book was a version of the interlace pattern in the centre of the Blue rug (Figs. 34 and 35) which was seen in one of the period rooms at the Victoria and Albert Museum.

Very often it is possible to borrow an Oriental rug and browse over it at leisure—people are generally most kind and willing to lend a treasure to a genuine student of rugs.

FIG. 33 *"Forest" rug in Surrey stitch on 10s canvas, designed and worked by G. V. Mathews. Size 31 × 63 inches.*

Hardly second to the rugs themselves as a source of inspiration are the pictures of the Old Masters, and those who admire and revere what is beautiful in the past and are wanting to produce something of lasting value in the present, cannot do better than visit picture galleries and note the rugs that appear in some of the great paintings. This source of design is enlarged upon in Chapter Nine.

Fair Isle patterns and designs for cross stitch, particularly those in the well-known D.M.C. (Dollfus-Mieg et Cie, Mulhouse) books, can all be used, but discrimination is needed when considering them as it must be remembered that cross stitch as such *embroiders* material and is not intended to *cover* it. The outside shapes of cross stitch motifs can first be drawn out, then "outlined", when alterations necessary to adapt them for rug purposes will often leap to the eye. What must be avoided is the small pattern which would probably look charming on a cushion or table-cloth where the material showed up the embroidery but which would be lost on a rug.

Suitable freehand outlines of possible patterns can be traced, and then transferred to squared paper, after which it is a simple matter to "square" the outline. Children's picture books often provide good line drawings of animals that can be used in this way.

Tessellated pavements in excavated Roman villas (there are very good postcard reproductions of those at Bignor in Sussex) and mosaics generally will suggest many ideas; borders can be adapted from pottery and textiles and certain types of leaded glass windows could be worked up into all-over patterns—in fact sources of design to help those who "cannot draw" are legion if they have the eyes to see.

Outlining

The outlining mentioned above is an all-important feature in the design of a rug. When studying Oriental rugs it will be noticed that practically all the motifs are outlined, generally with a contrasting colour but sometimes with a darker shade of the colour used for the motif itself. This outlining brings to life the colours and patterns outlined in an astounding way and it should be made an almost invariable rule. More will be said on this point in Chapter Eight.

One-colour Rugs

Occasionally a rug is necessary in a room where a much-patterned carpet seems to preclude a patterned rug—although a rug with a plain border and a simple design in the field, introducing a motif or two from the carpet, would produce a pleasant result and indeed enhance rather than detract from the beauty of the carpet itself.

A one-colour pile rug is extraordinarily dull to make and can show no individuality whatever, but interest can be given both to the working and to the finished rug if, instead of pile, a combination of flat stitches is used and, if possible, two or three shades of the selected colour. A difference in texture can add extra interest, e.g. if the very smooth Soumak stitch was worked in stripes alternating with the rather heavy rice stitch, or even with a pile stitch.

FIG. 34 *Blue rug in Surrey stitch on 10s canvas, designed by G. V. Mathews and worked by Sibyl I. Mathews. Size 31 × 54 inches.*

F IG . 35   *Detailed drawing of central interlace of Blue rug. One pair of hooks will be found to be shorter than the other—this was necessary to accommodate them in the space available in the width of the canvas.*

FIG. 36 *Striped rug in Surrey and Soumak stitches on 10s canvas, designed and worked by Mrs Mileham, with a motif of jet aircraft. In two shades of blue, two golds and dark brown for dividers. Size 27 × 53 inches.*

Adaptations

Probably the easiest way for beginners to start designing their own rugs is by adapting the actual patterns of other rugs, and for this purpose use can be made of the excellent portfolios of Swedish rug designs now to be had. These are shown in colour and reproduced on squared paper and nearly all of them are most effective. It will be noticed from the charts that the Swedish canvas differs from the English in that ten stitches in width equal seven in the length. This gives the worker an immediate opportunity for adaptation. If copied on English canvas from the Swedish charts most of the patterns would look very different and develop a peculiar flattened appearance.

Striped Rugs

Striped rugs are the simplest to work out when it comes to experimenting with individual designs, and five differing examples of this type of rug are illustrated.

1. A rug worked entirely in Interlocking Gobelin stitch. The stripes are of varying width and in three colours, dark cherry red, grey and a little blue. It is worked with Wilton 2-ply wool on 4s double mesh canvas. Fig. 29, page 67.

2. A rug worked in Surrey and Soumak stitches, giving a ribbed effect by using alternate pile and smooth surfaces. It is in two shades of blue and two of gold, with a small amount of dark brown to give "point" to the design, and is worked with Wilton 2-ply wool on 5s double mesh canvas. (Fig. 36.)

It should be noted that when using pile and flat stitches combined, the flat stripes must be of an appreciable width or they will disappear under the pile when the rug has been in use for some time, and the whole effect aimed at will be lost.

3. A child's rug worked in cross stitch, rice stitch and long-legged cross stitch. Animals in rows (taken from a Cartier-Bresson cross-stitch booklet) form the main stripes. It should be noted that the direction in which the animals face is reversed in the centre of the rug. The main background is "off-white", the other colours used being brown, red and green-blue. The animals are small so they are outlined in back stitch instead of cross stitches which would have looked somewhat clumsy. The rug is worked with several lengths of Brussels thrums (although two lengths of 2-ply thrums would have served the same purpose) and on 5s double mesh canvas. (Fig. 37.)

4. This rug appears primarily in order to show how the edging stitch should be worked in relation to the rest of the rug, but it also shows a change from the "straight rows" type of stripe. It is worked with 2-ply thrums on 4s single mesh jute. Fig. 7, page 37.

5. A rug in several flat stitches:

   (*a*) Striped ends in Interlocking Gobelin in dark and light green.
   (*b*) "Divider" stripes in dark green in long-legged cross stitch.
   (*c*) Diamonds outlined in a darkish green rice stitch, with centres of five gold rice stitches, and the rest of the diamonds filled with long-legged cross stitch in different shades of green, which stitch is also used, but in a reversed direction, as a background for the diamonds.

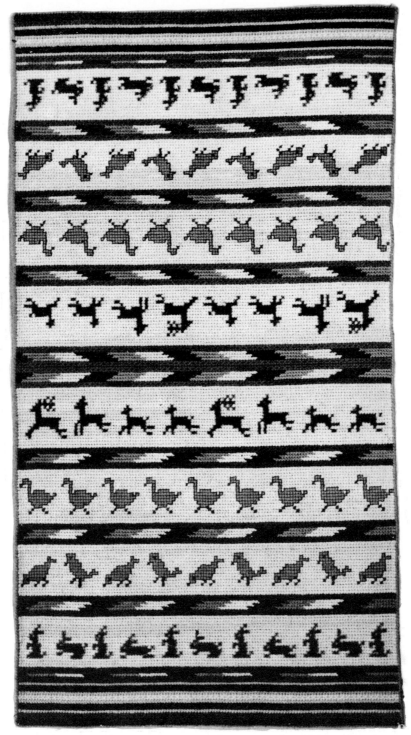

FIG. 37 *"Animal" rug in cross stitch, rice stitch and long-legged cross stitch on 5s canvas, Worked by Lady Aston; animals from a Cartier-Bresson cross stitch leaflet. In blue-greens, reds, browns, off-white. Size 27 × 47 inches.*

FIG. 38 *Green striped rug in rice stitch, Interlocking Gobelin and long-legged cross stitch on 5s canvas. Worked by G. V. Mathews. Six shades of green, small amount of gold. Size 27 × 47 inches.*

It is worked in 2-ply thrums from a mixed bundle of greens (apart from the gold) and on 5s double mesh canvas.

The rug is an exercise in various shades of green, this "kind" colour being chosen as it was designed to be made by someone suffering from eye trouble. (See Fig. 38, above.)

"Modern" Type Rugs

For those who prefer a type of rug in keeping with some present-day ideas of furniture, four suggestions are given.

Figs. 39 and 40 are, to all intents and purposes, plain rugs with the surfaces broken by a few lines—thirty-nine being in squares and forty in diagonal lines.

Fig. 41 has a plain border in which it is suggested that two of the sides should be worked in a different shade from the other two, e.g. two shades of brown. An alternative border could have two sides narrower than the other two sides.

Fig. 42 is an arrangement of interlaced oblongs. These have been worked in very bright colours on a dark cream background and many different colour arrangements are possible. The rug has a plain dull fawn border which could be omitted if desired.

Rugs with Borders

After these simple beginnings come rugs with borders, when as a general rule both border and the "field" (i.e. the part within the border) of the rug are decorated. On looking at

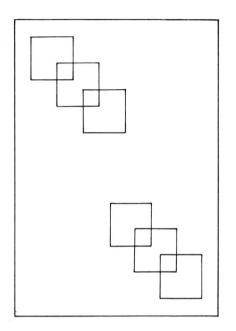

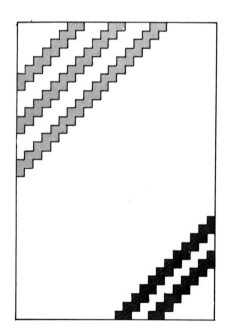

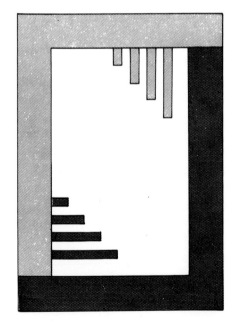

FIGS. 39, 40, 41   *Sketches for three very simple rugs.*

FIG. 42   *Chart for a rug with a design of interlaced oblongs.*

F<small>IG</small>. 43   *Rug in Soumak stitch on 7s canvas, designed and worked by Lady Aston.   Rust red with small amounts of blues, off-whites, reds and yellows.   Size 33 × 58 inches.*

classic examples, particularly the Caucasian and Bokhara types, it will be noticed that the designs are frequently based, in the main, on simple geometric shapes—squares, oblongs, diamonds, hexagons and octagons.

The border is all-important as it forms the framework to the field of the rug and should hold the design together. It should be of the same width all round the rug and about one-sixth of the total width of the rug. Therefore, a rug which has 120 stitches in its total width including the border should have about 20 at each side and 20 at each end as border. Naturally this can be varied within a few stitches, and some beautiful rugs have quite a small field within a border of many stripes, but a rug always looks well proportioned if the above general principle is followed. When wide borders result from this count they can, with great advantage, be divided into two, three or more stripes one of which should be more important than the others.

Many of the illustrations show examples of bordered rugs with designs based on geometrical shapes.

1. Fig. 43. This Soumak rug consists entirely of an arrangement of very simple shapes, chiefly diamonds, and is an excellent example of how these can produce a very attractive result.

2. Fig. 2, page 22. The Farmyard rug has as its focal points three eight-pointed stars surrounding a geometrical figure with a cross inside it, the whole enclosed in a "doodled" medallion. The rest of the field is filled with animals and geometrical forms arranged in a go-as-you-please way.

3. Fig. 34. The Blue Surrey rug has a more balanced design, the main shapes being halved at the sides of the field and quartered at the corners. Parts of the interlace motif appear also at the sides of the rug and at the ends, the whole plan being held together by the arrangement of the hooks. It should be noted that the conventional flower in the main border "meander" (Fig. 44) is of the same shape as that of the two large medallions (Fig. 45) and also that the tiny motif just inside the "tooth edge" repeats the same shape yet again. This relationship between the motifs in the field of a rug and its border helps to ensure a balanced design. (A meander is a serpentine figure embodying leaves or other motifs. It is a very natural type of border which can fill easily both narrow and wide border stripes and is therefore used extensively when designing rugs.)

4. Fig. 30. The Red Soumak shows a rather more elaborate development of a basic idea. This time the three main medallions are repeated in halves and quarters at the sides and corners as in the Blue rug, but there is a subsidiary medallion (similar to the one in the centre of the Farmyard rug) repeated twelve times, with background detail to enhance it, so that the rug is really designed as a repeating pattern of twelve. It should be noted that each of the "worms" in the background is curved in an "S" in order to key up with the repeating "Ss" in the border.

Examples 3 and 4 could, of course, be repeated as required to form a large carpet.

Colour

One of the great difficulties facing the rug maker is the fact that the majority of wool sold as "rug" wool tends to be dyed in harsh colours and in very few shades of any one colour.

FIG. 44 *Chart of meander from Blue rug and three other motifs.*

FIG. 45 *Chart of medallion from Blue rug.*

This is particularly true of nearly all the makes of thick wool, but more attractive colours and a greater variety of shades are to be found in mixed carpet thrums and in 2-ply wool of definite colours.

Generally speaking the finer the wool the better the colours available, and rug makers would indeed be happy if they could buy rug wool dyed in as many lovely colours as are obtainable in crewel wool and, to a somewhat lesser extent, in Brussels thrums. An ideal plan for fine rugs is to combine the inexpensive Brussels thrums with small amounts of crewel wool if needed for special colours, and this scheme has been followed for most of the fine rugs illustrated. In the Forest rug (Fig. 33) the touches of pale yellow, pale pink, pale blue and one of the greens are of crewel wool although the complete amount would not be more than one ounce. As strands of Brussels thrums and crewel wool are so similar in thickness they can be used together in the needle (see "shading", page 89) with good effect.

Faced with this colour problem many rug makers resort to home dyeing and if the results are somewhat unexpected so probably will the rug gain in interest. Many of the commercial dyes are very reliable and the rug maker is not hampered by the necessity of repeating the colour exactly between one batch of dyeing and the next. Within reason the more shades that result from using one coloured dye the more attractive will be the rug. A good supply of off-white wool is naturally best for such experiments, but a bundle of dull and uninteresting colours can all be lumped together in, say, a dark brown dye and will prove very useful for outlining.

Vegetable dyeing is more entertaining than using "packet dyes", but not everyone can cope with the amount of work, space and mess involved in this occupation.

It is obvious that colour in rugs is governed very much by personal choice, but experience (often by trial and error) has taught that:

1. As rugs are floor coverings they must withstand dirt, so that strong, rich colours are better than pale shades.

2. A restful effect results if one colour predominates, and up to two-thirds of the field of the rug can be worked in this colour or its near shades with advantage.

3. Some of this main colour in the field should always be introduced into the border. This helps to weld the border and field into a co-ordinated whole as does a link between the field and the borders as regards the design. See Blue Surrey rug, pages 76 and 85.

4. The same depth of tone throughout the rug is advisable, but in any case the border should never be lighter than the field. If it is, the picture looks liable to drop out of its frame.

5. A little of some dark colour in addition to dark outlining is generally effective—it helps to throw up the design.

6. Black should be used with great discrimination. Generally speaking very dark brown produces far better results than black would do, and for outlining it is always better to use dark brown rather than black.

7. The "high lights" to be used must be planned with care; they are of great importance but should not dominate the rug. As with design, the trained artist and those born with a sense of colour have advantages over the amateur; so again the advice for the novice or

rug maker who is not sure of his or her colour sense, is—study Oriental rugs and note the colour combinations used. It must be remembered that with old rugs the colours have generally faded and were much brighter when the rug was made, so when consulting a rug as regards its colouring both the back and front should be studied. Having done this when planning a particular rug, the scheme finally worked out is sure to end up as something quite different from that originally envisaged although the first ideas will be embodied in the final plan.

It is unwise to lay down any hard and fast rules as to what colours should be used and what should be avoided. Some rug makers can work in colour combinations that would be most uncomfortable if used in a less ingenious way. It is nearly always wise to introduce a small amount of a "funny peculiar" colour into an otherwise sober colour scheme, and conversely some neutral, dull colour to tone down a scheme otherwise possibly too bright. Contrast is just as desirable as harmony but needs greater skill in its use.

8. It will be noticed when studying Oriental rugs that they are frequently worked in very few colours but with many gradations of those colours. This example can be followed with great advantage.

9. Striped rugs look best with a wide stripe at each end of a dark tone, preferably darker than any other stripes in the rug, and forming, in effect, end borders. (Some people like to work a rug with only end borders and the rest of the rug plain.) Bright, strong colours are particularly effective for striped rugs and the balance of colour and width of the stripes must be considered with care. The colours should repeat themselves from the centre of the rug and a wide central stripe is recommended.

10. Outlining of patterns has already been mentioned and one of its chief advantages is the way in which it enhances the general colouring of the rug. A point of interest is that a light outline makes a given motif look much larger than does a dark outline.

Shading

Shading, i.e. the blending of two or more shades of one colour, is an important aspect of rug colouring, and the care with which it is accomplished makes a great difference to the finished appearance of the rug. In pile rugs a pleasant result follows if two near shades are used simultaneously in the needle. "Near" is the operative word, otherwise a spotted effect is produced.

With smooth-faced rugs two near shades should follow each other in the working but should not be used in the needle at the same time or again a somewhat spotty effect results. The lengths of wool in the needle should be varied so that the shades do not follow each other too regularly. As has been mentioned earlier, tent stitch when used lends itself particularly well to shading effects.

Chapter Eight

DESIGNING SPECIFIC RUGS

THE application of general principles is always easier if specific instances embodying them can be envisaged, so suggested schemes follow for designing (*a*) a slip mat and (*b*) a good sized rug.

The usual proportions for a rug which is not being made to fit into a particular space are for the length to be one and three-quarter times the width. It must, however, be remembered, when buying the canvas, that more will always be needed than for the theoretic finished length of the rug, to allow for the turn-over at each end and for variations in the working out of the design.

Slip mat on 5s canvas, finished size 18 inches by 32 inches.

This would make the mat 90 stitches wide and 160 stitches long.

It is wise, especially for the beginner, to use canvas in one of the usual widths so that there is a selvedge at each side. Joining *can* be done (see Chapter Ten) but it is laborious, so 18-inch-wide canvas is selected for this slip mat and 36 inch for the large rug as these widths are easily obtainable and suitable.

On the opposite page is a chart (Fig. 46) which should be studied carefully as it gives ideas both for borders and single motifs which can be built up to form simple designs.

The first point to notice is the way in which the outlining of the motifs enhances the general effect and also the method used for this. A curved or sloping line on a freehand design is first "squared", i.e. replaced as nearly as may be by a stepped line following the sides of small squares on the paper. The required outline stitches are then represented by such single squares or horizontal, vertical or diagonal rows of squares as have this stepped line for their inside boundary. In No. 15 on the chart leaves are shown in three stages, first drawn freehand, then squared and finally outlined. The pear and goblet motifs (Nos. 11 and 12), to be found in many Oriental rugs, and the conventional flower meander (No. 3), are also shown with and without their outlines. An outline is omitted in the tiny leaf meander (No. 8), both because this is somewhat small and delicate to take an outline and also because, when drawn as a subsidiary border for the Forest rug (Fig. 33) it was deliberately intended that it should be inconspicuous.

The procedure described above gives outlines of minimum thickness as shown on the chart and their importance cannot be over-estimated except where there are definite reasons for omitting them. If, on the other hand, it is desired to emphasise an outline still more, the first outline can itself be outlined by a second one.

Fig. 47 shows, for guidance and comparison, an outline of the same small subject incorrectly and correctly done.

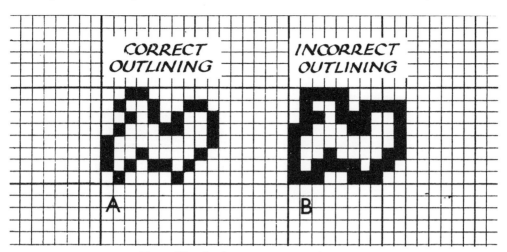

FIG. 47 *Outlining: correct and incorrect.*

The most usual ways of designing are:

1. Working out the complete scheme on graph paper, where one square of the paper will represent one stitch on the canvas.

2. Creating shapes and medallions by paper cutting. When cut, the resulting patterns can be placed on the canvas, adjusted for position, and a thread run round them to mark the shapes. Then when the paper is removed, the general effect and proportions can be seen. It is possible to get the main shapes in this way and to fill in the details either by eye or after drawing them first on graph paper.

3. Working in a completely go-as-you-please method. A few lucky people can achieve remarkably good results in this way (the maker of the Soumak rug, Fig. 43, does all her own designs by eye), but for the majority of people either method (1) or a combination of (1) and (2) ensures the most satisfactory finished design.

If it is decided to use method (1) it is necessary to start with a stock of squared paper (large sheets) as there is always a good deal of trial and error about all designing and several sheets will probably be needed before a satisfying result is finally obtained. On the whole paper with eight squares to the inch is the most convenient, although for a large rug 10s obviously uses fewer sheets of paper than 8s. The standard size for large sheets of squared paper is 22 by 18 inch, so that with eight squares to the inch, each representing a stitch, a single sheet is enough for drawing out any mat not more than 176 stitches in length or 144 in width. It is therefore ample for the slip mat now being designed (160 stitches long by 90 wide approximately).

A rectangle should first be ruled to represent the outside edge of the complete mat, to be followed by a line marking the inside edge of the border. A canvas 90 stitches wide will suggest a border about 15 stitches wide at both sides and ends. Actually 18-inch-wide 5s

FIG. 46 *Large design chart.*

canvas has generally only 89 (not 90) holes between selvedges and as the borders must be of equal width, this leaves an odd number of stitches for the field—say 59. As it happens that the majority of attractive designs for the field seem to involve points or corners (represented by single stitches) coming on centre lines of the design, such an odd number of stitches in the count is usually an advantage. In any case if the design should demand an even number it is easy to take two warp threads out of one of the selvedge sides to gain the extra stitch. (If Soumak stitch is to be used the extra stitch to be allowed for in the width (see pages 65–6) must not be forgotten.)

The border design should be considered first as the exact size of the field (both width and length) depends upon how this is worked out. A simple plan is advisable as it is a mistake to attempt an elaborate pattern for a narrow border in coarse canvas.

The "dividers" referred to in the table below are a necessary adjunct to all borders. Generally they should be worked in a dark colour to show up the various border stripes. Their use can be studied in many of the rugs illustrated.

Although only 15 to 17 stitches are available it would make a more attractive framework if the border was sub-divided, and five suggestions using patterns from the chart are tabulated below:

A   Outer edge   1 stitch
      Tooth edge   5 stitches (1) on chart
      Divider   1 stitch
      Small leaf meander   9 stitches (8) on chart
      Divider   1 stitch
                        Total width of border = 17 stitches.

B   Outer edge   1 stitch
      Spot pattern   5 stitches (9) on chart
      Divider   1 stitch
      Colour bands in 3s   3 stitches (2) on chart
      Divider   1 stitch
      Spot pattern   5 stitches (9) on chart
      Divider   1 stitch
                        Total width of border = 17 stitches.

C   Outer edge   1 stitch
      A line of single stitch spots between
          two plain lines   3 stitches
      Divider   1 stitch
      Wave pattern   5 stitches (4) on chart
      Divider   1 stitch
      Single spots between two lines as before   3 stitches
      Divider   1 stitch
                   Total width of border = 15 stitches

D	Outer edge	1 stitch
	Divider	1 stitch
	Colour band	2 stitches (10) on chart, three colours, two deep only
	Divider	1 stitch
	Barber's Pole	8 stitches (7) on chart, using 8 instead of 10 stitches
	Divider	1 stitch
	Colour band	2 stitches (10) on chart as above
	Divider	1 stitch

Total width of border = 17 stitches.

E	Outer edge	1 stitch
	Colour bands	5 stitches (5) on chart
	Divider	1 stitch
	Diagonal cross	7 stitches (6) on chart, using 7 central stitches only
	Divider	1 stitch

Total width of border = 15 stitches.

All these little border patterns "corner" quite easily but should any difficulty arise a small mirror placed upright on the pattern at 45 degrees to the drawing will show how the corner can be turned and is a most useful aid for designing.

Having decided upon a border (and many permutations and combinations can be worked out even from this one chart) it should be drawn out in detail, thus showing the exact size of the field.

It is unnecessary labour to colour charts in full (although shade indications may be given if desired) but for the sake of clarity it is advisable to paint in the outline stitches—see the black lines or single squares in the charts illustrated.

Colour ideas for these small borders depend chiefly upon the main colour selected for the mat, but there is no doubt that a line or two of something really dark—brown, blue, red, green—on the edges and between the stripes as dividers holds the whole design together.

In the single spot pattern used in (C), the spots could be in alternate off-white and medium brown between very dark brown lines.

The alternate (i.e. plain) diagonal bands in the barber's pole pattern could be in the main colour of the mat; so could one-half of the tooth edges.

It is while the design is being worked out that subsidiary colour ideas simmer and take shape, adding vastly to the interest of the experiments.

The field of the slip mat will be about 59 stitches wide and 130 long, (depending upon the border) and it will now be helpful to rule two lines lightly in order to show the centre point. When the number of stitches in the width is odd, the true centre line along the warp direction will pass through the middle of a row of squares on the paper, and instead of drawing this, two lines should be ruled enclosing this central row of squares between them. The same procedure should apply when the number of stitches in the length is odd. If both numbers are odd there will thus be four "centre lines" enclosing a single central square between them.

For a small field one, two or three medallions are suitable or, alternatively, an all-over pattern.

1. One plan is to decide upon a reasonable size for a centre medallion, mark where the outside lines of this would come to give good proportions to fit the field (working from the centre point), and then to "doodle" a quarter of an oval medallion outline. It is amazing how the pencil will travel over the paper given an idea of the shape to be produced. If preferred a paper shape can be cut, the prospective size having been marked on the paper first.

Fig. 48 is a suggestion for such a central medallion and it will be noted that the outline is four stitches wide. Extra importance can be given to medallions by making their outlines of an appreciable width.

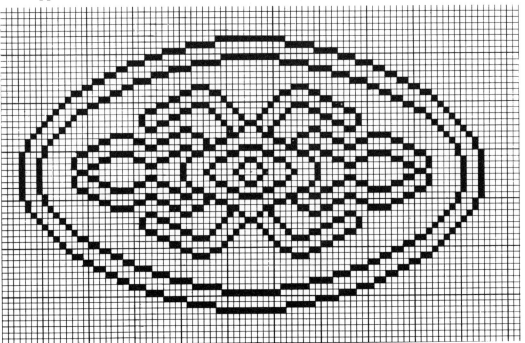

FIG. 48 *Medallion for a small rug.*

2. If three smaller medallions are preferred to one, use could be made of the shape shown in Fig. 49, page 95, and an interesting colour variation would be to interchange the colour of the pattern and its background within the medallion in the middle one of the three. The two shades of the medallion outline can also be interchanged with attractive results. Naturally there must be a good contrast in colour tone between the medallion outline and the main background of the field or the former will not show up clearly.

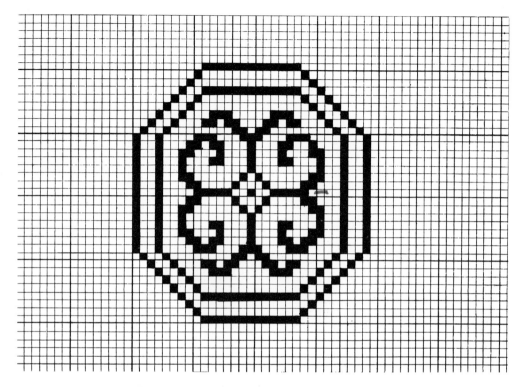

FIG. 49 *Alternative medallion for a small rug.*

These medallion patterns are given as suggestions only and are *not* correct sizes for the slip mat under discussion.

3. The pears and goblets illustrated (Nos. 11 and 12 on the chart), can be used to produce an all-over repeating pattern, as can many other suitable motifs. As an example the pears have been worked out in detail to fit this particular field, i.e. 59 by either 129 or 134 stitches.

Each pear (including its outline) is 20 by 13.

There can be six pears in the length and four in the width.

Length

Six pears long	120	Six pears long	120
Background—2 between each pear	10	Background—1 between each pear	5
Background—2 at each end	4	Background—2 at each end	4
Total length =	134	Total length =	129

Width

Four pears 13 wide	52
Background—1 between each pear	3
Background—2 at each side	4
Total width =	59

Various experiments can be made also with the goblets to make them fit into the field, such as using them in pairs (with or without the dividers) with the bases facing each other; with a divider between each pair, etc.

4. As well as the all-over detached motifs a good type of design for the field of a rug is a connected repeating pattern, such as simple geometrical shapes joined together. A suggestion for such a one is shown in Fig. 50. It is essential that this type of pattern for the field should be symmetrical about both its centre lines so that the two sides and the two ends should match when the pattern reaches the border. It is also very desirable that the borders should mark the completions of exact wholes or exact halves of units of this (or any other) repeating pattern.

It may be of interest to those who hunt for ideas in unlikely places to know that this particular one was derived from leaded window panes during a rather dull conference.

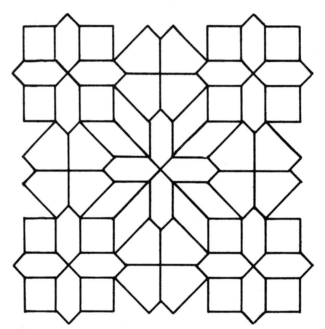

F IG . 50 *Repeating pattern taken from a leaded glass window.*

Creating Shapes by Paper Cutting

In order to make these shapes symmetrical the paper should be folded twice, giving four thicknesses of paper. The edges are then cut in steps to represent roughly one, two or more stitches on the canvas and these steps will be reproduced four times when the paper is unfolded. It should be noted that cuts made along the two sides, which show the four edges of the paper, will form the shape of the outside of a medallion, while cuts along the two sides having folds will form a pattern in its centre. The piece of paper falling from this last cutting—which will of course be of the same shape as the centre outline itself—can be used as another pattern unit. Newspaper is a very convenient form of paper to use for this method of creating shapes, as the lines of type and column dividers are helpful as guides when cutting the steps, and it is surprising what interesting results can be achieved in this way.

Large rug 36 inches wide by approximately 63 inches finished length

On 5s canvas the count will be about 180 by 315, and if 7s is used for a rather more ambitious and exciting rug, then there will be about 252 by 441 stitches.

The respective border widths should be, theoretically:

1. For 5s canvas, 30 stitches.
2. For 7s canvas, 42 stitches.

Although the general principles are the same, whether the rug be large or small, the large ones naturally involve rather more difficulties, particularly as several border stripes will be desirable, one, or possibly two, of which should be wider and more important than the others.

One of these wide borders could, with advantage, consist of detached devices, as in the main border of the Soumak rug, Fig. 43. This is one of the simplest forms of border, as, once the shapes of the motifs have been decided, nothing has to be done in the way of working out except to adjust the spaces of background between them in order to ensure that a motif comes symmetrically in each corner. In this adjustment an occasional variation of one stitch, either plus or minus, will not show.

With this Soumak rug the outer border is also, to all intents and purposes, formed by detached motifs, and here the adjustments are made by lengthening or shortening the joining lines, again with the object of making the pattern fit at the corners.

The Memlinc rug (Fig. 60) illustrates another example of the detached motif method of planning a border. The correct spacing of the hooks is ensured by juggling with the dividers between them, these being two in some places and one in others. In the narrow outer border the spacing required between the blue motifs worked out at three stitches except that one additional stitch was needed in the length and this was added at the centre point.

A border meander with a conventional flower evenly spaced as the chief unit is extremely useful. It can be adapted in various ways and is suitable for a wide border stripe. On the design chart (Fig. 46, facing page 91) a simple form of this is drawn in detail (No. 3 on the chart) to show how such a repeating pattern can be "cooked" to fit the corners of the width without in any way detracting from the symmetry of the design. Starting from the left end it will be seen that the flower repeats in 37 stitches and that there are three more repeats with one extra flower, viz. at the right-hand corner. As designed, this border needs 165 stitches made up as follows (reading from left to right):

Background	1 stitch
Four repeats of 37	148 stitches
Extra flower	15 stitches
Background	1 stitch
Total=165 stitches	

There are, however, only 163 stitches available in the width and the two arrows on the chart show where the two surplus stitches can conveniently be "lost". It might, of course, be necessary to gain these instead of losing them, when additional stitches could be added to the stem instead of being subtracted.

For the two rugs under discussion this type of meander, 17 stitches wide, would suit the 5s canvas (requiring a border of about 30 stitches wide) with the addition of two narrow stripes, while the 7s canvas (requiring a border about 42 stitches wide) would take it plus, say, a stripe of detached motifs about 12 stitches wide and two narrow colour bands.

The main border of the Blue Surrey rug (Fig. 44) shows a somewhat elaborate version of this particular meander.

With a rather more intricate wide border stripe, such as the oak leaves in the Forest rug (Fig. 51) or the double S pattern in the Red Soumak (Fig. 30), it will probably be found that the length of each repeat cannot be varied very greatly without destroying the effect desired, e.g. if the repeats in the oak-leaf border were increased or reduced by many stitches this would spoil the shape of the leaves, they would become either too elongated or too stumpy. In planning the Forest rug this border stripe was originally intended to form the outer, main framework of the whole rug, but, as it could not be adjusted satis-factorily to fit the number of stitches in the width of the canvas in that position, it had to be placed as the inner main stripe where the amount of adjustment required to make it fit happily was slight.

When planning the border of the Red Soumak rug, the double S type of design was considered suitable and attractive for the main stripe. This consists of a heavy S and a light S in reverse, and the actual length of the repeat is one that can be adjusted easily within moderate limits by varying the length of the light S. It was found that using a heavy S of 28 stitches and a light one of 23 (making a repeat of 51), with an additional heavy S to make the whole stripe symmetrical, four repeats fitted the width of canvas comfortably in its required position. In this case the corner turn does not carry through as in the oak-leaf border, but part of the open S is used at each corner to form a mitre (45 degrees) with a gap of a few stitches of background between them.

Having decided upon the design for the main border stripe or stripes and placed them satisfactorily, the remainder of the border width can be made up of any of the narrow borders discussed in connection with designing the small rugs. There are, of course, literally dozens of these to be seen when looking at good rugs, and imagination can produce many others.

When a meander (or other intricate pattern) is used for the main border stripe its design must first be arranged to fit the *ends* of the border and to provide for satisfactory turning of the corners since, unlike the length, the width of the rug cannot be adjusted. Naturally allowance must be made for any border stripes that may be outside the proposed meander. The subsequent fitting of the design to connect the corners along the sides of the border, while maintaining the continuity of the design, is almost certain to need adjustment in the length of the rug, assisted if necessary by such slight adjustments between repeats of the pattern as have been illustrated above. The need for starting with a rather longer length of canvas than might otherwise be thought necessary for an intended length of rug will now be apparent.

FIG. 51   *Oak-leaf border from forest rug; another idea for a border, and a motif.*

The complete border should now be charted on squared paper. A plain dividing line, preferably of two stitches, should always be added inside the border, this giving a clearly marked finish to the framework of the field.

The number of stitches in the width and length of the field should now be counted and faint lines ruled on the chart to determine the centre point or stitch finally.

Next the type of field must be considered, if this has not already been done when first planning the rug. The most usual types of pattern for this are:

1. One large centre medallion, an example of which is shown in Fig. 52, page 101. An attractive use has been made of detached motifs in order to fill most of the rest of the field of this rug, and an alternative filling could have been to use the quarters of the medallion in the corners with fewer detached motifs. The initials forming part of the decoration in the centre are those of the friends for whom this rug was made as a very personal gift.

2. Two or three medallions which could be halved at the sides and then quartered at the corners, see Figs. 30 and 34. This gives the effect of a frame having been put down on a small part of a large carpet covered with repeating medallions. The remainder of the field can be left plain or filled (*a*) with odd detached motifs as in the Blue Surrey rug or (*b*) with secondary repeating medallions which are surrounded by detached motifs as in the Red Soumak wherein the design is a repeat of twelve.

3. Repeating medallions throughout, either isolated or joined with lines through their centres as in the Elephant's Paw design mentioned in Chapter Nine. The Forest rug is of this type as is also the Memlinc, although the latter has a heavy dividing line between each medallion instead of the more usual background decoration.

4. An all-over repeating pattern as suggested for the small rug, although of course on a larger scale.

For all these types of design, both as a general help in charting and also in order to make the space to be filled looked somewhat less formidable, it is recommended that faint lines be ruled as guides for placing the main motifs. For instance:

1. *Single medallion type.* Four lines might be drawn in addition to the centre lines, to show the desired limits of the length and width of the medallion.

2. *Two medallions.* Lines would be drawn across the field half-way between each end and the lateral centre line, the centre point of each medallion coming where these lines cross the longitudinal centre line of the field.

3. *Repeating medallions.* Where there are, say, six lines of three medallions as in the Forest rug (one of which is shown in detail at Fig. 53), the number of stitches in the length of the field should be divided by six and lines drawn across the field accordingly. There will, of course, be five lines. Similarly, the number of stitches in the width should be counted and divided by three, and two lines drawn lengthwise. These lines will enclose equal rectangles and the medallions should be placed symmetrically in these.

4. The method of placing an all-over pattern in the field has already been discussed in the case of the small mat and no further considerations apply to the larger rug.

It has been stated that an attractive rug can be made if a plain border is used with a

FIG. 52 *Rug with single medallion, designed and worked by Mrs Addison in Surrey stitch on 5s canvas. Size 27 × 54 inches. Mainly cream and a deep rust; smaller details in various colours.*

patterned centre, and the reverse is, of course, also the case. This means that any beginner facing the problem of designing a first rug can simplify matters either by planning a rug with a border design and a plain field or vice versa, and later have the pleasure of working out a design embodying decoration in both places.

Figs 44 and 51 show other ideas for borders and motifs, and many more will be found in the books listed in Appendix 2—Bibliography.

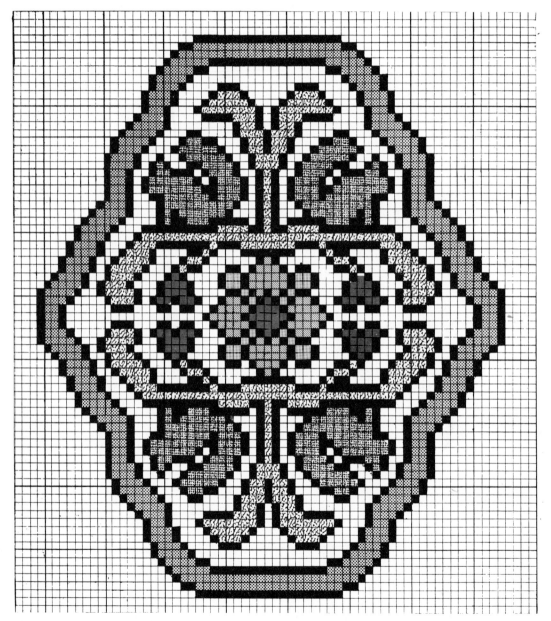

FIG. 53   *Medallion from Forest rug. The outline and "acorns" were in blue-green, the leaves green,
the squirrels dark fawn and the flowers red, blue and yellow.*

Chapter Nine

CHURCH RUGS AND CARPETS

SOME years ago it was my pleasure and privilege to see Winchester Cathedral through the eyes of a boy of sixteen with whom I spent several hours exploring its marvels. Rather to my surprise what seemed to impress him more than anything were the embroideries in the chancel; each stall and choir seat was examined minutely and it was difficult to entice him away when time became a matter of importance. As we walked from the West door, simultaneously we turned round to gaze once more at the towering Cathedral and the great buttresses flying heavenwards, and he broke the silence by saying suddenly: "I shall never forget those embroideries. The people who did them must have worked with the same spirit and ideals as those responsible for building the cathedral."

His words have remained with me vividly and have often come to mind when seeing the lovely work that has been, and is still being, done to beautify cathedrals and churches up and down the country. Whether it is the fine, elaborate work of the great cathedral guilds or the simpler efforts of the parish sewing party, the spirit behind the gift is the same and surely never has embroidery been more worth while in its accomplishment. A small village in west Wiltshire completed a hundred kneelers in a year. They were worked on rather a coarse "open" single mesh canvas and with single lengths of 2-ply Axminster thrums. The patterns used were simplicity itself and as a labour of love and worship the result is staggering.

In the embroidery world there seems to be somewhat of a cleavage between the devotees of freehand embroidery and those who prefer counted thread work with the discipline the method imposes. From the former come the altar linen and church vestments, from the latter the stall seats and kneelers in canvas work, and it is to those whose particular interest is counted thread embroidery that the idea of making rugs and carpets for their churches might appeal.

An interesting experiment is being made by the congregation of a small and beautiful church in the Chilterns. This had been "restored" about the middle of the last century and, among other embellishments, tiles had been laid all over the chancel and sanctuary floors in shades of tobacco brown, daffodil yellow and chocolate. The effect was devastating and members of a work-party engaged upon making exquisite kneelers in beautiful colours and designs realised that the effect of their work would be utterly spoilt if seen in conjunction with these tiles. The result of consultation with the architect interested in the church was a scheme to make large rugs using every conceivable shade of stone colour, worked in squares, and thus to cover the tiles wherever possible. One reason for making rugs for churches may thus be to disguise ugliness; at the other end of the scale it is to adorn further what is already beautiful.

Methods of workmanship, any of which would be suitable for church rugs, have been dealt with in full already, and the one selected would probably be a matter to be decided upon between the church authorities and the maker (or makers) of the rug.

In churches the most appropriate places for rugs would be on the altar steps, either directly before the altar itself or on the steps leading up from the altar rails; for the lectern platform, where a small rug would often be a most decorative addition; or for the steps leading into the pulpit. This latter position involves difficulties if the steps curve, although they can, with care, be overcome, but many pulpits possess steps with a right-angled turn which would present no problems.

If a very large rug was needed a co-operative effort would probably be made and a rug combining cross stitch, long-legged and rice stitches would be particularly suitable, as, apart from being pleasing in themselves, these stitches are practical when the question of joins comes into the picture—as they will surely do for a co-operative carpet. Obviously these joins must be very strong and as invisible as possible. (See Chapter Ten.)

Working in strips is an excellent plan where the rug is made co-operatively and makes for simplicity when, in the course of time, repairs become necessary. Rugs used in front of the altar will have their wear mainly in one place, viz. where the officiating priest stands, and one or more strips can be extracted, repaired and replaced if the rug has been worked in sections originally.

If a few knots (in pile rugs) or stitches (in smooth-faced rugs) wear out, these can be renewed without much trouble. Soumak rugs, however, although they will give years of hard wear before anything in the way of repairing becomes necessary, are tiresome to mend because of the difficulty of extracting a worn piece owing to the close interlocking of the stitches. To a lesser extent the same problem arises with tent stitch.

Two ideas are offered as suggestions for rugs in squares:

1. Fig. 54 is taken from a mosaic pavement and can be put to several uses.

(*a*) It could be a repeating pattern on a long, narrow rug, in which case the square containing the cross would form the left-hand end and it would be advisable that the same cross should appear in the square at the right-hand end.

(*b*) Fig. 55 shows how the repeating squares could become the border of a large rug. The arms of the mosaic cross shown would need to be outlined to look effective on a rug.

(*c*) Fig. 55 also indicates (by dotted lines) how the repeating squares could be adapted to provide an all-over pattern.

(*d*) The squares could be used also for a rug with end borders only.

Whether all, alternate, or only some few of the squares were filled with a symbolic or other suitable design would depend upon the arrangement used. The curl in the dividing borders makes an effective pattern in itself and over-elaboration in the squares should be avoided.

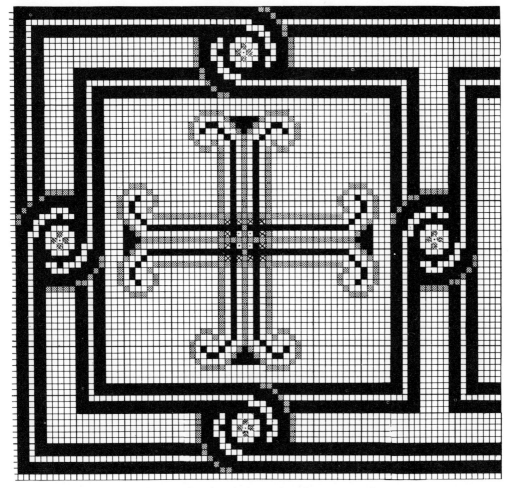

FIG. 54 *Design for church rug, taken from a mosaic pavement.*

2. Fig. 56 is based on vague ideas suggested by the colourful square panels on the beautiful roof of the nave in St David's Cathedral. The framework of the panels was decorated with V-shaped colour bands (such as are shown on the design chart, Fig. 53, number 5) but if this type of divider was used a large rug would be necessary in order to result in pleasing proportions, since using these bands entails a framework not less than 5 stitches wide. The embryo design in Fig. 56 shows plain dividers, 3 stitches wide, and various ideas for filling the squares are suggested; the three-leaf patterns being nearest to the design in the roof panels. These fillings can be arranged according to individual ideas as in the mosaic pavement design.

Either of these schemes could be utilised in making a rug with "arms" so that it would lie in front and on each side of the altar. A rug of this shape looks well in a church and enhances the importance of the altar, but its position, of course, can never be changed so the wear will come always in the same place. It will therefore need repairing more often than would an oblong rug that could be turned round frequently.

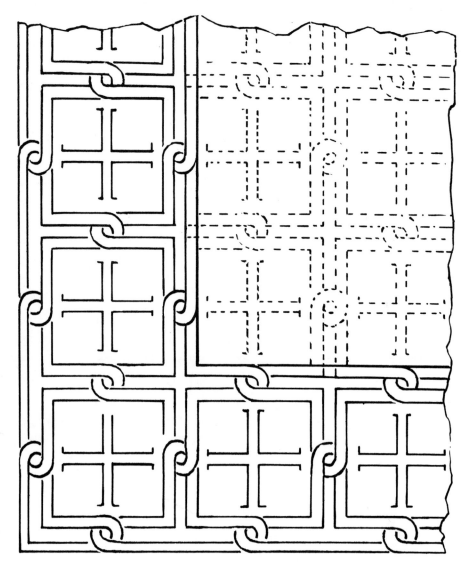

FIG. 55　*Suggestions for variations on Fig. 54.*

The general principles of rug design differ not at all when specialised rugs are envisaged but naturally the use of religious symbols springs to mind in connection with all work for churches. These symbols are innumerable: geometrical shapes such as the Cross in its various forms; the living and inanimate objects that so often typify a particular saint; animals; flowers; plants; letters; numbers—there is no end to the possibilities, but all must be considered with regard to their appearance when "squared"—and what their sizes would be on different canvases. (See Chapter Seven.) Every symbol selected must also be bold enough to show up well and be suitable for outlining.

FIG. 56　*Chart based on ideas from the roof of St David's Cathedr*

A few suggestions follow but the whole subject of symbolism needs detailed and specialised study if symbolic motifs are to be used extensively. See Appendix 2—Bibliography.

In Fig. 57 (an idea taken from an old stole) there are combined:

1. The Cross, greatest of all church symbols, which is surrounded by (2) the Circle, having no beginning or end and thus symbolizing Eternity, and (3) three intersecting circles which symbolize the Holy Trinity. This pattern would be very suitable for a long, narrow pile carpet before the altar rails, where sometimes a carpet is preferred to a padded kneeler. It would be a very easy design to use for co-operative work.

The palm and olive branches shown in Fig. 58 could be used in alternative ways:

1. The two branches could be placed side by side at each end of a long, narrow rug, each one being enclosed in a narrow framework.

2. They could be used as a border (a plain field is envisaged in both cases) although care would be needed in their spacing and it would be advisable to reverse the direction of the branches in the centres of both the long and short sides of the rug. (The branches are so drawn that they can be shortened or lengthened in order to fit any design.) A cross at each of the four corners would finish the border appropriately. As each square on the chart in this case equals 1 inch (5 stitches) the border, if using 5s canvas, would be 7½ inches to 8 inches wide, allowing for dividing lines.

It would always add interest to a carpet if the special emblem associated with the saint to whom the church is dedicated could be included in the design, but these must always be considered in relation to the medium of carpet making. For instance, St Cecilia's harp or St Lawrence's gridiron, with the many thin, straight lines involved, would look mean and almost certainly confused. A single line of stitches is practically always ineffective in a carpet.

Conversely St Benedict's raven, St Clement's anchor and St Jude's ship could all be used as motifs if made large enough.

Of great interest to rug makers are the marvellous and obviously faithful reproductions of Eastern carpets in the work of the great medieval painters, and when these pictorial representations are compared with comparatively modern Eastern carpets their family resemblances are most startling. Kendrick speaks of a painting of "The Virgin and Child" (in a gallery at Vienna) by Hans Memlinc (1433–94), where the main central pattern in the carpet depicted is almost identical with that of a nineteenth-century Caucasian carpet. Many of these famous pictures show exquisite rugs which are painted with such minute attention to detail that it is easy to pick out some of the motifs and recognise them as used in the rugs of today.

Certain moments when they experience breath-taking beauty are, happily, enshrined in the memories of many people. A visit to Bruges granted me such a moment when I was faced with Memlinc's "Mystic Marriage of St Catherine" and the world stood still during the half-hour in which I tried to absorb its loveliness. Naturally my enjoyment was enhanced by Memlinc's inclusion in the picture of a delightful rug spread beneath St

FIG. 57 *Design for narrow carpet for altar rails, from old stole pattern.*

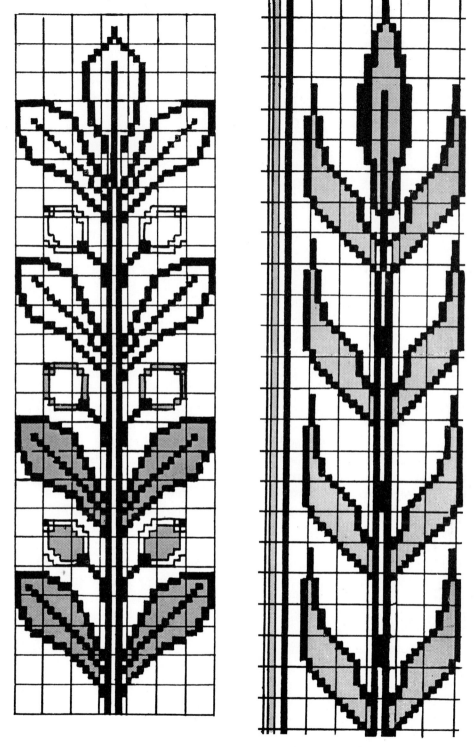

FIG. 58   *Olive and palm branches.*

Catherine's feet, and, luckily for me, peeping out well beyond them. Of course, something had to be done about that rug. A coloured postcard was sufficiently clear to be of real help in recalling the colours and basic lines of the design and now St Catherine's rug is also my own to some extent. Mine is not, of course, an exact replica—I should not wish it to be so —but it provides a tangible memorial of an unforgettable experience and the story is told in the hope that it may lead others to find ideas and pleasure in a closer study of pictures with a secondary object in view. It is an obvious advantage of this method of looking for inspiration that a great deal more of value is gained by close observation of such pictures than merely acquiring ideas for personal rug designs.

In the Appendix 1 there is a short list of pictures in which carpets are depicted and the galleries in which they can be seen.

Individuality will always tell and it is quite unnecessary to try to be too original in order to produce a satisfying rug. "In the long run it is not nearly so important whether the artist himself invents a motif as what he makes of the motif once it has come into existence" (Roger Fry)—and the fact that in the loveliest of Oriental rugs the same patterns appear again and again, and are handed down from generation to generation, shows that the Eastern rug makers realised that they had found what were completely satisfying basic ideas for their craft and were prepared to attain their individual results by superimposing their own idiosyncrasies upon these. No two Eastern rugs are ever twins, although many makers might use the same or very similar motifs.

One of the fascinating aspects of the study of old rugs is the development of the designs throughout the centuries. An elaborate version of the wheel on the rug in Memlinc's picture appears as part of a well-known Turcoman rug design some two hundred years later. Probably the more that paintings in which rugs are introduced are studied, the more such intriguing developments will be noticed.

As the last mentioned point is so well brought out in the alteration that time has brought in the two wheels, detailed charts are shown of both of them (Fig. 59). "A" is basically the wheel from the Memlinc picture, although somewhat simplified, and "B" is the very much more complicated form taken in detail from the back of a Turcoman rug. There are many variations of this particular design, which is known colloquially as the Elephant's Paw or Elephant's Pad, and the wheel shown was used in the main border pattern of a particularly beautiful specimen. Facing these wheels is a reproduction of the Memlinc picture of St Catherine, and the following page shows the rug, the design and making of which has given me such pleasure during the past year. Some rug maker whose parish church is dedicated to St Catherine could not do better than use the same source.

Colouring for church rugs will be dependent upon where they are to be placed, and it is particularly important to experiment with colour schemes and look at the results *in situ*, noticing whether the colours blend with their surroundings and pick up the other colours in the church in a happy way. Having selected the wool it is proposed to use, the experiment of throwing a bundle of these on the floor where the rug is to lie will be an invaluable aid to the final choice of colour and shade.

Light is all-important in the colour of rugs, and to bring a rug really to life it must have the correct light, but this may not be easy of attainment in a medieval church. In such a site the aim should be to ensure that the rug is in harmony with the other church decorations rather than that it is a focal point.

When designing a rug for a modern church very likely it will be found that particularly bright, clear colours are called for, and a design adapted from the Caucasian type would meet the purpose well. These rugs are vivid and with fewer gradations of colour than the Persian rugs, and the simpler type of design would probably suit its surroundings. It is wise to avoid the restless and uncomfortable result that is so often produced when a design is designated as "modern". Nothing is to be gained by being "modern" merely in order to be fashionable, which so frequently means discarding all that is old and of good repute. A well-worked rug, with a pleasing and restful design and carefully chosen colours, is the result of much forethought as well as an immense number of hours of actual stitching, and it should last for several generations. Therefore its design should not run the risk of being of an ephemeral nature.

With colour, as with design, the knowledge and experience of the East are available for all who have access to a good museum, and once again it cannot be too strongly emphasised that "the Oriental does not indulge in that wild striving after originality now so prevalent in the West" (Kendrick) but is content to follow tradition to a large extent. The rug makers of today, with a true sense of values, cannot do better than express their own individuality by building upon that which generation upon generation has accepted as being intrinsically beautiful.

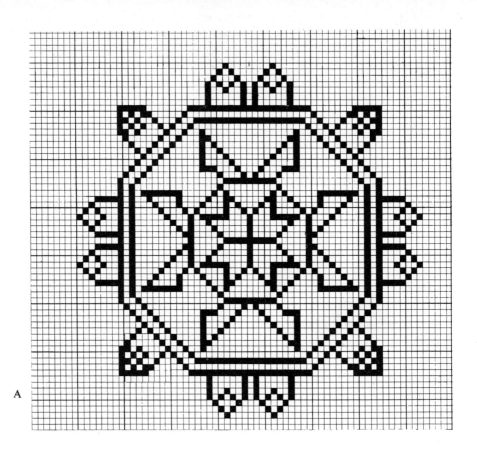

A

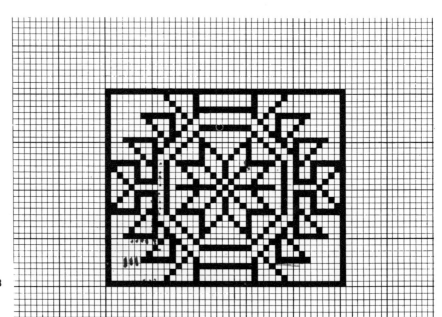

B

FIG. 59 *Charts of the Memlinc wheel* (above) *and "Elephant's Paw" motif.*

FIG. 60 *"The Mystical Marriage of St Catherine" by Hans Memlinc* (by kind permission of the Director of the Hôpital St-Jean, Bruges).

73
3
219

F<small>IG</small>. 61 *Memlinc rug in Surrey stitch on 8s canvas, designed and worked by Sibyl I. Mathews after the one in Memlinc's picture. Size 27 × 47 inches.*

Chapter Ten

JOINING AND FINISHING

JOINING can never be anything but tedious and somewhat difficult and it is much better to avoid it if possible. There are, however, cases in which it has to be undertaken, such as with a co-operatively worked carpet or a carpet made to fit a particular place. As an example of the former, a carpet has recently been made for the altar steps of Washington Cathedral, U.S.A., consisting of twenty-two separate pieces which have been joined together. (An illustration of this carpet appeared in the Spring 1959 number of *Embroidery*, the Journal of the Embroiderers' Guild.)

There are two methods of joining which are satisfactory—the overlap method which can be used for joins which run either horizontally across the width of the canvas, or longitudinally from end to end, and the selvedge method which, as its name implies, can only be used for a longitudinal join, i.e. along the selvedges. Properly made both types of join are extremely strong and a rough edge of canvas on the surface can be avoided when the rug is to be smooth-faced.

Method 1 (a). Joining two strips of canvas horizontally across the width of the rug by the overlap method—suitable for flat stitches only.

(i) Assuming that there are two strips to be joined and two workers, A will work her chart complete and leave eight unworked rows of canvas *below* her last line of stitching.

(ii) B will first rule a horizontal line on her chart eight rows from its top. Leaving six unworked rows at the *top* of her canvas, she will work the seventh row of her canvas with the design starting at the ninth row of her chart (the row below the ruled line) and complete the remainder of her chart.

(iii) The bottom two unworked rows of A's canvas should now be folded under and the canvas superimposed on B's unworked canvas for an overlap of four rows. There will thus be eight unworked rows of canvas (to be worked later) made up as follows, reading from top to bottom:

Two rows of single thickness on A's canvas
Two rows of two thicknesses where the canvases overlap ⎫ i.e. making up the
Two rows of three thicknesses where the canvases overlap and ⎬ overlap of 4
　A's canvas is doubled over ⎭ stitches.
Two rows of single thickness on B's canvas

These thicknesses will also apply to the selvedges but as the join is a strong one the double back of the selvedge where the three thicknesses occur can safely be snipped out.

The overlapped canvases must now be sewn to each other very carefully hole by hole, both on the upper and lower sides, viz. on the upper side where the fold of A's canvas rests upon B's (i.e. the edge of the three thicknesses portion) and on the lower side where the cut edge of B's canvas meets A's canvas underneath the latter.

(iv) The missing eight rows on B's chart (the rows above the ruled line) are then worked, thereby filling the empty canvas, completing the design and covering the join.

There will be an unavoidable thickening of the canvas where the three thicknesses overlap but there will be no rough edge on the surface.

Should it be desired to avoid having three thicknesses of canvas, this can be managed if more time and trouble are spent on the join. In this case it will be necessary for A to leave more than eight rows of unworked canvas below her completed work—say 12 rows. Instead of turning her canvas under for two rows she draws out six weft double bars (i.e. still leaving six double bars undrawn below where her work ends as in the previous method after the fold of two rows). The long protruding warp threads resulting from this are threaded downwards to lie side by side with the corresponding ones at the back of B's canvas and through the back of B's work. It is advisable to sew the overlap into position before doing this threading. This will result in a join of only two thicknesses of canvas which will be unnoticeable after the rug has been in use for a short time. Both methods are equally strong.

Method 1 (b). Joining two strips longitudinally along the length of the rug by the overlap method—suitable for flat stitches and pile.

(i) In this case the width of the canvas used must allow at least 8 more stitches between selvedges than the number across the width of the chart. Assuming that there are two strips and two workers, A will work her chart complete and leave a strip of unworked canvas 8 stitches wide to the right of her work after the right-hand selvedge (if present) has been cut off.

(ii) B will first rule a vertical line on her chart 8 stitches from its left-hand edge. Leaving a strip of unworked canvas 6 stitches wide in addition to the selvedge (if present) on the left, she will work all the design shown on her chart to the *right* of the ruled line. If there is a selvedge on the left side of the canvas it should then be cut off.

(iii) A strip of A's unworked canvas 2 stitches wide should be folded under and A's canvas then superimposed on B's for an overlap of a strip 4 stitches wide.

(iv) The sewing of the join and completion of the work across it has already been described under 1 (*a*).

If it is desired to reduce the join to two thicknesses, the threading method already described can be used, though it is of course the warp threads which will be drawn out and the weft threads threaded in and no selvedges will be concerned in the join.

It should be noted that it is inadvisable to use a pile stitch when the join is across the width of the canvas (method 1 (*a*)) owing to the extreme difficulty of inserting the last row when completing the design after joining. Pile stitches can, however, be used with method 1 (*b*), and in this case there is no need to fold A's canvas under as the cut edge will disappear into the pile. Both A and B will in this case leave strips of unworked canvas 6 stitches wide (instead of A leaving 8 stitches to allow for the fold under) and these strips are superimposed for an overlap of 4 stitches and sewn together as before.

Method 2. The selvedge method of joining.

In this method the right-hand selvedge of one and the left-hand selvedge of the other of the two pieces to be joined are bent sharply towards the underside of the canvas just at the last selvedge warp threads where the sewing holes start. The last selvedge threads of the two pieces are then tightly sewn together so as to form in effect a double bar of what should appear to be a continuous piece of canvas with two selvedge edges projecting from it at the back.

Since the two threads sewn together form a double bar, the chart must show an extra stitch where this type of join is to be used. If, for instance, there are 90 double warp bars on each piece of canvas the chart must show a total of 181 stitches.

If A and B are the workers of the two strips, A's chart will show one more stitch in the width than B's. Both A and B should stop work three rows short of the selvedges to be joined and the latter should then be joined as above. If all has been done correctly there should be 7 double weft bars left to be covered (including the one at the join), viz. 4 from A's chart and 3 from B's.

It is essential that the sewing together should be done very firmly, the greatest care being taken to ensure that corresponding holes in each piece of canvas are exactly in line as otherwise the join will show.

The two pieces having been firmly sewn together in the correct position the missing rows of 7 stitches are worked over the join to complete the design.

Finally the two edges of selvedge are splayed out under the rug and can, if desired, be sewn down to the back of the work.

It should be noted that those stitches in which the wool at the back of the canvas lies parallel to the selvedge are the simplest to use when a join is made by this method, e.g. long-legged cross stitch, but pile can be used if care is exercised.

As in any case the joining of worked strips is a somewhat intricate operation, it is obvious that a better finish will result if one expert worker is in charge when a co-operative carpet entails joins.

Finishing Rugs

The appearance of the majority of rugs is improved if they are stretched, and with smooth-faced rugs it is vital to do this.

The first essential is an expanse of clean, bare boards larger than the rug itself. The corner of a little-used bedroom floor, where the rug can be left undisturbed for some time, is ideal.

1. With the rug face upwards, tack one of the long sides along the line of a floorboard. The tacks should be spaced about 2 inches apart and the side tacked should, at this stage, be stretched only just enough to make it lie flat.

2. One of the ends (the longer one if by any ill chance these are unequal) must now be

tacked so that it is held at right angles to the long side already tacked. This **may** need some pulling in order to get the end in its correct position and perfectly straight. The tacks should again be about 2 inches apart.

3. Pull (if need be) and fix the remaining corner so that the second end when tacked will lie at right angles to the first side and will equal the first end in length.

4. Tack the second side and end so that both are held in straight lines. Some force may be required to accomplish this.

5. Insert extra tacks so that they will be about an inch apart. If enough tacks are not used the edges will curve inwards between the tacks and these curves will show in the finished rug.

6. Place sheets of clean blotting paper all over the rug, take a large sponge and a basin of cold water and *soak* the blotting paper with as much water as you can make it hold—and then a bit more. Most people are inclined to be frightened and do not use enough water.

7. Cover the whole affair with a piece of blanket or an old bath towel, after first laying strips of brown paper over where the lines of tacks come to avoid rust marks on the bath towel, etc. and leave it alone for at least a week.

As regards slight rust marks on the rug itself, these will not show if the edging is dark, (as is normally the case), or if the edging is not worked until after the stretching process is over (as recommended for all smooth-faced rugs, see page 37). The rug must be absolutely dry before the tacks are removed when the result will both astonish and please. Should this not be the case it will probably be for one of two reasons—either that not enough water was used to impregnate the rug or that it was not allowed to dry sufficiently before being taken up from the floor.

Lining

Rugs should never be lined. A sewn-on lining adds to the weight and is liable to pull the rug out of shape. Any grit, dirt, or tiny stones that may fall from rubber-soled shoes on to the surface of a rug will pass through it without doing any damage, if it is unlined, and can be swept up when the rug is lifted. Anyone cleaning a room and moving a rug knows how much dirt collects beneath it, and it is better beneath than held by a lining within the rug itself where the grit will tend to break the threads of wool.

If a non-slip backing is required, an open mesh rubber material (rather like wire mesh netting) can be bought cut to any size desired and this can be laid on the floor and the rug placed on top of it.

Fringes

The value of the addition of fringes to needle-made rugs is a debatable question.

All loom-made rugs must have fringes since when the rug is finished and cut off the loom the warp threads are left loose and of course the whole rug would disintegrate if they were not securely fastened together. A knotted fringe is an obvious way of dealing with the matter, and while a rug is still comparatively new it looks well; but what owner of Oriental rugs has not suffered from the fringes of any such rugs they may possess fraying and becoming unbearably untidy? Even without animals in the house to hasten the process (and cats and dogs both enjoy nothing more than playing with the fringes of rugs), continual daily wear and tear invariably causes the fringes to need repair while the rest of the rug is still in good condition. Of course a vacuum cleaner should never go near an Oriental rug but in practice it often does so. That being the case, and as a fringe serves no practical purpose, there seems little point in adding it to a rug that is not made on a loom. A well worked plaited edging stitch is so pleasing in itself and shows off the rug to such advantage that any other finish is in the nature of a work of supererogation.

Chapter Eleven

TALKING AND TEACHING

Talking

ONE of the pleasures of learning any craft is the probability that it will ensure the making of numerous new acquaintances, many of whom will become friends. Sometimes it is rather a difficult problem to decide whether or not to work at a rug or piece of embroidery in an hotel lounge or railway carriage as the odds are that it will soon mean the end of a peaceful "sew"—someone is sure to want to know "how to do it". This gives one an insight into a beginner's problems (and also their enthusiasms) and these trial trips are helpful when the moment comes for talking about rugs to a Women's Institute, Towns-women's Guild, Young Wives' Club, etc. It is amazing how many such bodies exist today, and all of them want talks on a great variety of subjects of which the practical crafts are among the favourites.

Nothing will teach the rug maker more about her craft than accepting some of these invitations, but before talking about a hobby to an audience it is obvious that the speaker must:

(*a*) have many examples of work to show as illustrations for the talk;

(*b*) be competent to answer innumerable questions;

(*c*) be prepared to demonstrate how a particular stitch or stitches should be worked, and

(*d*) almost above all, know how to control an audience when, as is inevitable, many individuals among it will not be particularly interested in the subject put before them—a quarter of those present may have asked for a talk on rugs but the attention of the other three-quarters must be held too and, if possible, fired with a desire to learn.

(*a*) The first item on the list is the one that takes the time, as building up a collection of rugs is not a rapid occupation although an absorbing one, but nothing made will be wasted as all experimental efforts make good talking points. People can learn much from the mistakes of others, and for the speaker to point out where she has gone wrong in design, colour or workmanship is worth a lot to the audience.

It helps to make a talk particularly interesting if it is possible to show examples of rugs, however small, worked on various types and sizes of canvas. Therefore, when starting a new rug, it is a good plan to see if it can be made slightly different in some such way from others in the collection. Many rugs will have anecdotes connected with their inception and making, and mentioning these generally interests an audience.

(*b*) Answering questions can be a pleasure, as from them the speaker often gains a new angle upon her subject; but it is of course absolutely essential that she herself should know that subject from A to Z if Question Time is to be enjoyed. When a question is put to which the answer is not known the wisest plan is to admit ignorance and to ask the questioner for her name and address, saying that the answer will be sent by post. However knowledgeable the speaker may be, this problem arises on occasions.

(*c*) Very often members of an audience appreciate being shown how to work a stitch that has been used on a rug that particularly appeals to them, and if this can be demonstrated it is a popular move—especially for those who are having to listen to the talk whether or not they are interested in the subject (and have only come for the cup of tea and social chat that generally ends such gatherings). A large piece of the very open mesh single thread Helvellyn B quality canvas, or the coarse, white-with-blue-lines, 3s double mesh canvas, tacked to a wooden frame, is recommended for this. Probably those who are really interested will gather round afterwards and ask for more instruction, and it has been found worth while to be prepared for this by having half a dozen small pieces of canvas, wool and needles handy, so that people can experiment for themselves. Personal experience has shown that it is in such small ways that rug makers are born—one rug maker was started on her way by being shown how to work Surrey stitch by a friend leaning out of a railway carriage window and demonstrating the knot on a small piece of canvas as the train started to move.

(*d*) Although holding the interest of an audience seems to begin and end with real knowledge and enthusiasm on the part of the speaker, one or two suggestions may be useful.

1. An attractive display of small rugs, samplers, books, charts, etc. arranged to catch the eye helps to rivet attention on the talk.

2. The rugs should never be examined until the talk is finished; if they are handed out during the lecture the attention of the audience will be lost for good.

3. The audience should be kept guessing and the talk worked up from the simplest beginnings to the party pieces—in fact the marzipan should be kept to the end. The audience will soon realise that better and better objects are being produced from the lucky bag and become more and more interested in consequence. A large suitcase kept behind the table where the display has been set up, with the rugs to be shown arranged in it in the order in which they are to be produced, is a most valuable asset. It is impossible to travel "light" when on rug expeditions.

4. To emphasise what has been mentioned before, it seems to make for a particularly happy audience-lecturer relationship if people are told of mishaps and mistakes and are allowed to see these and share in the speaker's adverse criticism of her own work.

5. A very obvious point—but it is surprising how often speakers neglect it—a firm eye should be kept on the clock. Extra time can be given in the question period and it is as well to leave people wanting more rather than to let them feel satiated. Sometimes speakers are inclined to trail off and the audience is not quite sure whether the talk has finished or not, so a telling sentence or an applicable quotation as a final touch is useful in producing an effective full close.

Teaching

Very often a talk leads to a request for classes and the rug maker is given the pleasure of passing on her own knowledge.

Many of the points already mentioned apply to teaching also, with a few additions which are small in themselves but may help to ensure happy and successful classes.

1. As not all the members of the class may have heard the original talk, a short run through the rug collection at the first class will arouse interest in newcomers and re-arouse it in those who have seen the rugs before.

2. This short introduction should be connected up with the syllabus that has been sent out already to the class members before the course begins, so that everybody knows exactly what is expected of them.

3. One member of the class should be asked to act as a class secretary to deal with all monies, registers and such matters. An efficient class secretary helps the teacher enormously.

4. Everybody should be encouraged to start by making a rug sampler upon which they can work all the stitches that are taught. The value of such a reference book for individuals has already been suggested in Chapter Three but it is absolutely essential for class work.

5. Apart from showing finished rugs illustrating the particular stitches to be taught at any one lesson, it is a great help to the pupils if they are given (or rather lent) small individual samplers with examples of these stitches worked upon them, singly, in groups and in little patterns. The samplers should be marked clearly with the teacher's name and address by sewn-on tapes—this for obvious reasons. Of course it takes a long time for the teacher to prepare these samplers but they can be used over and over again and the rapid progress made by the pupils when they can each handle this very personal visual aid, and compare their own work with it, is most rewarding.

6. If, before handing out these individual samplers, the stitch is demonstrated before the whole class, everyone starts off with at least an idea as to what they are aiming to produce. In a class of twelve students some will be able to work the stitch after this demonstration, others will need more personal help. Nearly all members of the class will have individual difficulties which may seem trivial to the teacher who knows the subject so thoroughly but which are nevertheless real snags to the pupils. The wooden frame with a piece of canvas stretched across it, mentioned earlier, is useful for general class demonstrating, so also is a portable blackboard. A very good version of this latter is the "Unique Surface", which is backed by pliable strong canvas mounted on rollers, and is supplied by Wilson and Garden Ltd., of Kilsyth, Glasgow. Lines representing the rug canvas can be specially ruled on this surface by the makers on request, either to show double mesh or single mesh canvas, and if the inside of the squares is, say, $1\frac{1}{2}$ by $1\frac{1}{2}$ inches they can be seen clearly at a distance. Different coloured chalks are recommended for use with these blackboards—and a green surface can be obtained instead of black if preferred.

7. As it should be possible for anyone to start on a rug after four lessons, six lessons makes a satisfactory short course, and it has been found to be a good plan to have the first three or four classes in consecutive weeks and the last two at fortnightly intervals. This

will mean that the rugs should be progressing well before the course ends, and when this is the case there is less chance that they will be tucked away when once the enthusiasm engendered by the course has waned and other interests have supervened. A rug cannot be designed and worked in a few hours. If 5s canvas is used 27 inches wide and of 50 inches finished length, that will mean 250 rows. An average time for working each row would be just over three-quarters of an hour, which means very nearly 200 hours' work for the finished rug. If the class members can be induced to form themselves into a rug club and have regular meetings they will all help each other.

8. Rug makers are inclined to fall into two categories, those who start on coarse rugs, find them completely satisfying and continue to make these; and those whose ambition drives them to try something finer and so produce for themselves a rug with much of the characteristic beauty of its Eastern relations, only made at a fraction of the cost. In all rug courses, mounted samples of all types of canvas and wool, as well as the finished products, help pupils to decide what to attempt, but for first samplers it is wise to work either on double mesh 5s canvas or on the 4s single mesh jute. The former (see Chapter Two) is definitely easier for certain of the more elaborate flat stitches, and suits the eyesight of older people better than the jute, but the latter is very easy to handle, being pliable yet strong. For experimental purposes samples of fine canvas should be available for pupils with ambitious leanings.

9. In all classes there are apt to be a few pupils who find difficulty in keeping up with the pace of the majority. These are inclined to get worried and if the teacher can stay a little later than the official time for closing the class and give these one or two a few minutes' individual attention after the others have gone, this will pay good dividends. Those taking up new learning when not so young, are inclined to get "fussed" in a crowd, but a little peaceful extra tuition will often solve their problems and start them happily on their way.

Everyone who has tried to teach to others what is of absorbing interest to herself knows that there is no occupation more rewarding and enthralling, and the greatest rewards of all are when the laggards catch up with the hares—and often emulate the tortoises—or when a pupil says: "I never bothered to look at rugs before these classes and now I cannot keep my eyes off them."

This chapter is not for TEACHERS but for those teachers (in very small letters) who may find themselves drifting or being "pitchforked" into that most fascinating of occupations with little or no preparation. A personal experience some twelve years ago of such a beginning with all its difficulties, is the reason for offering these notes with the hope that they may be of use to some people.

Even now there are possibly those who would like to teach and yet find that they are, through some cause, unable to take advantage of the tremendous help as regards training that can in these days be sought and found by consultation with the Town or County Further Education authorities. To these, an emphasis on what has been learnt by experiment of the value of personal touches may not come amiss.

Appendix 1

PAINTINGS DEPICTING RUGS

SOME famous pictures in which enough of a rug appears for it to be valuable as an idea for working out an individual design.

National Gallery

Hans Holbein the Younger (1497/8–1543). *The Ambassadors.*
Gerard Terborch (1617–81). No. 864. *The Guitar Lesson.*
Gabriel Metsu (1629–67). No. 838. *The Duet.*
Carlo Crivelli (1430?–95). No. 739. *The Annunciation of St Emidius.*
Hans Memlinc (1433–94). *The Donne Triptych.*
Hans Memlinc (1433–94). No. 686. *The Virgin and Child with an Angel, St George and Donor.*
Joos van Ghent (about 1435–75). No. 756. *Music.*
Giovanni Bellini (1428?–1516). No. 3911. *The Virgin and Child Enthroned.*
Lorenzo Lotto (1480–1556). No. 1047. *Family Group.*
Pinturicchio (1454–1513). No. 703. *The Virgin and Child.*
Master of St Giles. No. 4681. *The Master of St Giles.*
Ochtervelt. No. 2553. *A Young Lady Trimming Her Finger-nails.*
Cornelisz Duyster (*c.* 1599–1635). No. 1387. *A man and woman playing trick-track, and three other men.*[1]

National Portrait Gallery

Hans Holbein (attributed to). *William Warham.*
Paul van Somer (1570–1621?). *Francis Bacon, Viscount St Albans.*
Marc Gheeraedts the younger (1561–1635). *Somerset House Conference of 1604.*[2]
Artist unknown. *George Villiers, first Duke of Buckingham.*

Tate Gallery

Marc Gheeraedts the younger. *Third Earl of Downe.*
Marc Gheeraedts the younger. *Lady Aston.*

Wallace Collection

G. Metsu (1628–67). *The Letter Writer Surprised.*
G. Terborch (1617–81). *The Lady Reading a Letter.*
Hendrich Gerritsy Pot (1585–1657). *Ladies and Cavaliers at Cards.*
C. Netscher (1639–84). *A Lady Playing the Guitar.*

[1] A very good reproduction. The carpet is reputed to be Turkish.
[2] An excellent and very clear reproduction of a large table carpet. Lovingly painted carpets appear in so many of Gheeraedts' pictures that one sometimes wonders whether he can have chosen carpets as his first interest and then looked round for "sitters" to go with them!

National Gallery of Scotland
Attributed to P. Oudry. *Mary, Queen of Scots.*

MANCHESTER
Art Gallery
John Souch. *Thomas Aston at the Deathbed of his wife (1635).*

LIVERPOOL
Walker Art Gallery
William Hogarth (1697–1764). *David Garrick as Richard III.*
Hans Holbein, School of. *Henry VIII.*

BRISTOL
City Art Gallery
Ambrogio da Predis (active 1472–1506). *Francesco Sforza as a Child.*

BIRMINGHAM
Art Gallery
Jacob Ochterveldt (late seventeenth century). *The Music Lesson.*

NOTTINGHAM
Art Gallery
Artist unknown. *Charles, Lord Howard of Effingham, first Earl of Nottingham.*

BRUGES
Museum
Jan van Eyck (1380–1440). *The Virgin with St Donatien, St George and Donor.*

This list is not, of course, exhaustive and mentions but a few of the pictures to be seen in British galleries wherein rugs are depicted. Tracking down others will provide an added interest to rug enthusiasts visiting picture galleries.

Being ignorant of foreign galleries (except in Bruges) I am not competent to speak of their treasures, which are legion.

At the Victoria and Albert Museum the table carpets should not be missed. The most famous example of such a one is that from the collection of Lord St John of Bletsoe, Melchbourne Park, which dates from the mid-sixteenth century and is one of the earliest specimens of a tent stitch carpet.

At the Birmingham Museum is the Mary Holte table carpet, which is another fine example of a table carpet.

In the Witt Gallery of the Courtauld Institute, Woburn Square, London, W.1, there is ample opportunity to study rug designs in the files of Flemish masters and also in the book by Ganz on Holbein.

Appendix 2

BIBLIOGRAPHY

1. *Hand Woven Carpets*, 2 vols, Kendrick and Tattersall.
   This is a stupendous work. One volume contains coloured plates and one the letterpress. It is a mine of fascinating information but is only to be found at large libraries.

2. *A History of British Carpets*, C. E. C. Tattersall, (F. Lewis).
   A valuable book of reference and most interesting reading. It can be borrowed on request from branches of public libraries.

3. *The Rug (Le Tapis)*, Albert Achdjian, (Editions Self, Paris).
   This book is printed in both English and French, is full of superb illustrations, many in excellent colours, and has reproductions of numerous small pictorial motifs which are a source of inspiration for designing. It is, unluckily, expensive, £2 10*s*., "remainder" price, but is well worth the initial cost for serious rug students. Can also be borrowed from public libraries.

4. *How to Identify Persian and Other Oriental Rugs*, G. J. Delabere May (G. Bell & Sons). 16*s*.
   A very useful and inexpensive book with numerous helpful illustrations.

5. *How to Know Oriental Carpets and Rugs*, Heinrich Jacoby (Fisher & Unwin). 21*s*.

6. *A Practical Book of Oriental Rugs*, G. Griffin Lewis (Lippincott, U.S.A.).
   Can be borrowed from public libraries.

7. *Notes on Carpet Knotting and Weaving*, C. E. C. Tattersall, (Victoria and Albert Museum). 2*s*.
   A "must" for all rug makers. It is invaluable in many ways and amazingly inexpensive.

8. *Dictionary of Embroidery Stitches*, Mary Thomas, (Hodder & Stoughton). 10*s*. 6*d*.
   A comprehensive work on embroidery stitches generally including many that are suitable for rug making.

9. *Ecclesiastical Embroidery*, Beryl Dean, (Batsford). £2 10*s*.
   A book that should be consulted by those making rugs and carpets for churches—many valuable references to the use of symbolism.

10. *Bulgarian Folk Embroidery*, Rossitsa Choukanova. (Imported from Bulgaria by John Pinder-Wilson & Partners). £2 10*s*.
    An expensive book but containing many patterns that could be adapted for rug making.

11. Portfolios 2, 6, 10 Lts. Forlag, Stockholm. 15*s*. 6*d*. each.
    Good designs for adaptations. The Tiranti Bookshop, 72 Charlotte Street, W.1, and Miss K. R. Drummond, 21 Little Russell Street, London W.C.1, stock these portfolios. *Oriental Rugs*, Hermann Haack, tr. G. & C. Wingfield Digby, (Faber & Faber). 30*s*.

12. Many of the D.M.C. publications are useful when looking for ideas for designs.

Appendix 3

SOME SUPPLIERS OF MATERIALS

In U.K.

Mace & Nairn, 89 Crane Street, Salisbury, Wiltshire (wide range of canvas)
Jackson's Rug-Craft Centre, Croft Mill, Hebden Bridge, Yorkshire
Loomcraft, Southside, Headcorn Road, Sutton Valence, Kent
The Needlewoman Shop, 146–148 Regent Street, London W1R 6BA
The Royal Wilton Carpet Factory, Wilton, nr. Salisbury, Wiltshire
Spinning Jenny, Bradley, Keighley, Yorkshire
The Winwood Textile Co., Lisle Avenue, Kidderminster, Worcestershire
Reginald Parker & Co Ltd., 46 George Street, Ayr
Harrods Ltd., Knightsbridge, London S.W.1

In U.S.A.

WHOLESALE SUPPLIERS

(write them for names of stores nearest you)

Boye Needle Co, 4343 N Ravenswood Ave, Chicago, Ill. 60613 *Needles*
Emile Bernat & Sons Co, Depot and Mendon Sts, Uxbridge, Mass. 01569 *Canvas, Needles*
Paternayan Bros. Inc, 312 E 95 St, New York, N Y 10028 *Canvas, wools, needles*

RETAIL SUPPLIERS

(they will fill mail orders)

Alice Maynard, 558 Madison Avenue, New York, N Y 10022 *Canvas, wools, needles*
Merribee Needle Art Co, 2904 W Lancaster St, Fort Worth, Texas 75107 *Canvas, wools*

Index